Influencer Marketing Mastery Secrets

2 book in 1 Tips and Tricks, How to Reach a million Followers through Social Media such as Instagram, Facebook, Twitter and YouTube in the New Age

JASON MILLER
&
RAY ROBBINS

@ Copyright 2020 - All rights reserved

The content contained whiten this book may not be reproduced, duplicated or transmitted without direct written permission from the author or the publisher.

Under no circumstances will any blame or legal responsibility be held against the publisher, or author, for any damages, reparation, or monetary loss due to the information contained within this book. Either directly or indirectly.

Legale Notice:

This book is only for personal use. This book is copyright protected. You cannot amend, distributed, sell, use, quote or paraphrase any part, or the content within this book, without the consent of the author or publisher.

Disclaimer notice:

Please note the information contained within this document is for educational and entertainment purposes only. All effort has been executed to present accurate up to date, and reliable, complete information. No warranties of any kind are declared or implied. Readers acknowledge that the author is not engaging in the rendering or legal, financial, medical or professional advice. The content within this book has been derived from various sources. Please consult a licensed professional before attempting any techniques outlined in this book.

By reading this document, the reader agrees that under no circumstance is the author responsible for any losses, direct or indirect, which are incurred as a result of the use of the information contained within this document, including, but no limited to, errors, omissions or inaccuracies.

Table of Contents

INFLUENCER MARKETING

Introduction 11

Chapter 1:

Important Social Networks 14

    Important Social Networks -- 15

    Pinterest -- 15

    Instagram -- 16

    Facebook --- 17

    YouTube -- 19

    Snapchat --- 19

    Twitter -- 20

    Others --- 21

    Why Social Media Marketing Works ------------------------------- 21

    How to Use Social Media to Generate Profits -------------------- 23

    Going Viral --- 24

    Formats Used in Social Media Marketing ------------------------ 25

    What Is an Influencer -- 25

    How to Find Influencers -- 26

Chapter 2:

Brand Building on Social Media 27

    Choosing a Name --- 27

Logo Design --- 28

Colors --- 31

Consistency --- 31

Convey a Message or Be Abstract? -------------------------------------- 32

Convey Your Ideal Customer --- 32

Always Brand Your Posts -- 33

Making a Familiar Impression -- 33

Bio --- 33

Choose a Branding Font -- 35

Voice and Tone -- 35

On Social Media – You Have Seconds --------------------------------- 36

How Serious Is Your Brand? -- 37

Consider Multiple Accounts -- 37

Take Stock of Where You Are -- 38

Actionable Steps --- 39

Chapter 3:

Elements of a Good Post 41

Plan Ahead --- 41

Be Clear and Concise --- 42

Message Focus --- 43

Active Voice -- 45

Focus on Benefits, Not Features --------------------------------------- 46

Think in Terms of Building Relationships ---------------------------- 48

Give Away Valuable Information --- 49

Social Media Is Interactive --- 50

"Which is better. Red or white? And why?" --- 50

Start a Blog --- 50

Share News Related to Your Niche --- 51

Post Infographics --- 52

Always Link --- 52

Call to Action --- 52

Mix Things Up --- 53

How to Stimulate Curiosity --- 54

Special Requirements for Different Social Media Networks --- 54

Examples of a Good Post --- 56

Chapter 4:
Daily Actions and Overall Approach 58

Setting a Posting Schedule --- 59

Prep Time --- 60

Engagement --- 61

Don't Be Discouraged --- 61

Leveraging the Followers of Others --- 62

Leverage Quora --- 63

Chapter 5:
Instagram 64

Good Photographs --- 65

Simultaneous Posting --- 66

  Posting Procedure -- 66

  Helper Apps for Instagram -- 67

  Posting Frequency -- 67

  Your Link -- 68

  Instagram Business Accounts -- 70

  First Step: Build Up Some Content -------------------------------------- 70

  Trading Posts -- 71

  Paid Posting --- 72

  Be Ready for Traffic --- 73

  Summary -- 74

Chapter 6:

Facebook 75

  Setting up a Business on Facebook -------------------------------------- 75

  Creating a Facebook Page --- 75

  About Page --- 76

  Facebook Page Button --- 77

  Posting -- 77

  Advertising -- 78

Chapter 7:

YouTube 79

  Posting Frequency -- 79

  Video Length --- 80

Follow Examples ---- 80

The Thumbnail Image ---- 81

Setting Up Your Video ---- 84

Promoting Your Video on Other Sites ---- 86

Earning Money from YouTube ---- 87

Chapter 8:

Advertising on Facebook and YouTube 88

Facebook Advertising ---- 88

Audience Insights ---- 88

Ad Type and Goal ---- 90

Budget ---- 91

Media ---- 92

Platform Options ---- 92

YouTube Advertising ---- 93

Leveraging Videos ---- 93

Budget ---- 94

Chapter 9:

Passive Income 95

Work Now, Payoff Later ---- 95

Consistency Is the Key ---- 96

Free and Paid Traffic Leads to Passive Income ---- 97

Finding Offers to Sell ---- 98

Affiliate Marketing ---- 99

Chapter 10:

Sales Methods **104**

    Email Marketing -- 104

    Sales Funnel -- 105

    Driving Traffic --- 107

    Summary -- 110

Conclusion **111**

SOCIAL MEDIA MARKETING TRICKS 2020

INTRODUCTIONS 115

CHAPTER--ONE

SOCIAL MEDIA OR SOCIAL NETWORKS --------------------------117

    SOCIAL MEDIA TRACKING -- 117

    SOCIAL NETWORK METRICS --- 119

    STRATEGIES FOR SOCIAL MEDIA MARKETING ----------------- 121

    IDENTIFYING WINNING STRATEGIES FOR MARKETING ON SOCIAL MEDIA --- 127

CHAPTER--TWO

FACEBOOK MARKETING 2020... 147

    TIPS FOR SUCCESSFUL MARKETING STRATEGY ON FACEBOOK -- 162

    HERE'S HOW TO CREATE A POWERFUL FACEBOOK PAGE - 166

    OPTIMIZE POSTS ON YOUR FACEBOOK PAGE ------------------ 169

FACEBOOK MARKETING: GUIDE TO GET CUSTOMERS AND
SALES WITH A SMALL BUSINESS ------------------------------------ 174

HOW TO MAKE MONEY ON FACEBOOK PAGE ------------------ 181

CHAPTER--THREE

INSTAGRAM MARKETING 2020 .... **184**

HOW TO CUSTOMIZE YOUR INSTAGRAM? ----------------------- 188

TIPS TO GETTING FOLLOWERS ON INSTAGRAM ---------------- 198

HOW TO CREATE AN INSTAGRAM MARKETING STRATEGY
FOR YOUR BUSINESS --- 202

HOW TO OPTIMIZE ACCOUNT AND SELL ------------------------- 209

HOW DOES THE INSTAGRAM ALGORITHM WORK ------------ 211

HOW TO BEAT THE INSTAGRAM ALGORITHM------------------ 213

MONETIZING YOUR INSTAGRAM PAGE --------------------------- 219

CHAPTER--FOUR

YOUTUBE MARKETING 2020 .... **226**

STEPS TO CREATE YOUR YOUTUBE CHANNEL ------------------ 238

STEPS TO MONETIZE YOUTUBE VIDEOS -------------------------- 243

TRICKS TO IMPROVE YOUR YOUTUBE CHANNEL -------------- 245

CHAPTER--FIVE

TWITTER MARKETING 2020 .... **255**

HOW TO LEVERAGE TWITTER AS A MARKETING TOOL ---- 257

MARKETING ON TWITTER IN 2020 --------------------------------- 259

COMMON MISTAKES THAT ARE MADE ON TWITTER -------- 261

HOW TO CREATE YOUR LIST ON TWITTER ---------------------- 264

TWITTER ANALYTICS -- 266

HOW TO EARN MONEY USING TWITTER ------------------------- 272

CONCLUSION 277

Introduction

Congratulations on purchasing *Influencer Marketing,* and thank you for doing so.

The world has changed radically in the past decade. With the advent of social media and smart mobile phones, the media, communication, and marketing landscape was completely upended. It started early in the century with Myspace, which was quickly blown away by Facebook, which basically took their idea and did it much better. Meanwhile, YouTube was quickly becoming a popular website for watching videos, but it was dismissed as a silly pastime, where people went to watch funny "cat videos."

At first, Facebook almost operated under the radar. In the first few years, as it began growing in popularity, few realized the marketing power that the website had. Businesses were slow to notice and get on board. Everyone wondered how a website like that could make money. Nonetheless, the site kept attracting members and growing steadily.

At about the same time, the smartphone was invented, and Apple upended the world with the introduction of the iPhone, which was basically a handheld computer that had a phone in it. Again, at first, people didn't know what to make of it, and it seemed like an idle curiosity. About a year later, Apple then opened the app store. At first, people were putting a lot of games on the app store, and people didn't make the connection – what if you had social media on people's phones? At the time, a lot of hype surrounded the device, as individual software developers created rudimentary games that people could play on their phones, and many became instant millionaires.

This period introduced a whirlwind of change. Pretty soon, Twitter followed on Facebook, and other sharing sites like Pinterest continued growing. Perhaps observing Pinterest, some innovative entrepreneurs created Instagram, a simple app that allowed people to share photos with memes on them.

Fast forward to today, and you know the rest of the story. Now social media plays a prominent role in communication, marketing, and advertising. For business owners, social media has proven to be one of the most powerful tools available. Not only is social media powerful, but it levels the playing field.

If you are a small business or just an individual who is hustling online and looking to get customers, social media has opened up the world's markets to access in ways that have never before been possible.

In this book, we are going to help explain how small businesses and individual entrepreneurs can exploit social media to grow their business and sell products. Reaching the public has never been easier, and different market segments can be targeted, often for free, and if not for free, at a low cost.

In this book, you will learn the most important social networks and what influencer marketing is and how that offers another channel that you can use in order to reach customers. And, as you will see, you can become a small "influencer" yourself, simply by putting out regular content.

After we come to understand Facebook, YouTube, Instagram, and other social media networks, we will investigate branding. You will learn simple and easy to implement tricks that can be used to brand yourself and create a presence on social media, which can turn into profits. We will explore the daily actions that you must take in order to build a following that will turn into actual profits.

As a part of your education, you will learn how to create effective social media posts. These posts can be put up as free posts, or used in paid advertising campaigns.

Then we will explore the idea of a sales funnel. Although the internet and social media has evolved rapidly, some of the same techniques still work. Among these is the concept of an email list and a sales funnel. One of the powerful ways that social media can be used with a small business is to push traffic to your sales funnel. If you have an effective sales funnel, it is not difficult to turn this traffic into profits.

YouTube is a great social media website; in fact, it may be one of the best. If you are able to use video to share content, it is relatively easy to build a large following and drive significant traffic from YouTube to your social media sites, and your sales funnel.

Finally, we will talk about paid advertising on Facebook, YouTube, and Instagram. Paid advertising is surprisingly low cost and powerful on social media websites. Simple advertisements on Facebook that cost only a few dollars a day to run can drive a lot of traffic. If you are going to pursue Facebook, advertising, you better be ready for the traffic! We will also talk about using YouTube and exploiting popular videos to get people's eyeballs on your products. YouTube advertising is similarly surprisingly inexpensive.

There are plenty of books on this subject on the market, thanks again for choosing this one! Every effort was made to ensure it is full of as much useful information as possible, please enjoy!

Chapter 1:

Important Social Networks

Welcome to the world of social media. In the past ten years, the communication landscape has been completely transformed. Although the old media is still around and frankly as big as ever, the attention of people is now split between many different communications technologies. And this is very good news for small businesses. The days of three network television stations and a couple of radio stations, which required a massive advertising budget to get any airtime, are long gone. In their place is a dynamic and easily accessible landscape where you can get followers and new customers without spending any money, and if you do spend money, you can use targeted advertising without breaking the bank.

The power to do targeted advertising is one of the most important reasons why your business should be on social media. You can zoom in on any demographic, location, or interest that is related to your business and your ideal customer. If you don't yet know your ideal customer, advertising on networks like Facebook is a great way to find out who they are.

The problem for many people in small business is they don't really know which social networks they should be using to reach their prospective audience. Second, they aren't sure how to reach that audience, even if they have some idea which social networks are the most powerful. We hope to demystify these issues in this book. Let's get started by looking at the most important social networks that you should be using to focus your attention.

Important Social Networks

Social media has become incredibly diverse and fractionated. However, the major stalwarts remain where the action is. In our experience, Facebook, Instagram, and YouTube are King. In fact, these social media networks are so important that you could devote all of your time to using these networks, and you'd get all of the results that you want for your business.

That said, there are many social networks that can also be leveraged to bring in new customers. But which ones are really worth bothering with? The first thing is that it depends.

Knowing who your ideal customer is will be one of the central things that you need to keep in mind with your business. Of course, you already knew that because everyone in marketing knows how important that concept is. When you know who your ideal customer is, then you can target them more easily and effectively.

The first thing you want to think about is what gender are you marketing to. Is your customer base primarily female, male, or a fairly good mix of the two? How old is your typical customer? Are they 25, or 65? These are important things that need to be taken into consideration when using social media as a part of your marketing plan, because people of different ages, on average, can be found in different places. Let's take a look at the demographic data of some of the social media sites and apps.

Pinterest

If you read a lot of books on social media marketing, many of them are going to hype up Pinterest. And with good reason. According to the web traffic sit Similar Web, last month, Pinterest had an astounding 848 million visits. The bounce rate, which tells you how many people only look at one page and then leave, is about 43%, which is a pretty decent value. So, it sounds like you should be on Pinterest!

The reality is that it depends on what your business is about and who you are trying to reach. Let's start with gender. According to the Omnicore Agency, 70% of Pinterest users are female. The trend has become a little more balanced in recent years, with 40% of new signups actually being male users, but that still leaves men in the minority on the site. If you are marketing products that are of interest to men or to both genders, then Pinterest is not something you should be wasting your time on. On the other hand, if you are targeting young adult females, Pinterest might be exactly where you want to be.

Among active users, females are three times as likely to be an active user as compared to a male. And they trend young. Some 34% of Pinterest users are aged 18-29, and 28% are 30-49. Only 17% are 65+. So, if you are advertising hearing aids, trying to do it on Pinterest is probably not the ideal course of action. But if you are selling shoes for women made in hot colors – it might be exactly where you want to be.

Instagram

Interestingly, Instagram also trends female, although the demographics are far more balanced. Some 52% of users are female, so there is a slight imbalance. In the United States, it is estimated that 43% of adult females use Instagram, and about 31% of adult males use Instagram. Overall, 110 million Americans are on Instagram, and some 130 million users will tap on a shopping post to learn more about a product. A large fraction of American users, some 63%, look at Instagram at least once a day.

If you aren't on Instagram with your business, you're already late to the party (but don't worry about it, it's never too late). It's estimated that 25 million U.S. businesses have an Instagram account. The app is extremely popular with so-called influencers, with surveys showing that nearly three-fourths of them list Instagram as their preferred social media site. The total possible reach on Instagram is 800 million people worldwide.

One of the factors that has made Instagram such a success is the fact that it's a mobile application rather than a website. Now you can reach Instagram through a website, but the overwhelming majority of users access it through the app. Why is this important? Because an app is something you always have with you since people are glued to their smartphones. An app also makes it easier to check, rather than jumping on a desktop computer to find out what is going on with some website. People still use desktop and laptop computers, of course, but an app just makes it easier for them to access. An app is also good for advertisers. Instagram is a simple visual medium where you can post images with a message or short 15 second videos. This opens up great marketing tools for small businesses.

Instagram opens up a little more of an older audience than Pinterest does, but 72% of teens are on Instagram, and only 31% of those aged 18-24 use it. Not sure why there is such a large drop-off, people who are aged 18-24 were young when Instagram came online about 8-9 years ago, you would think they would be completely accustomed to it.

In any case, the numbers are quite large – meaning it's worth utilizing for many businesses. Wouldn't you like to have instant access to 31% of 18-24-year-olds?

Facebook

Facebook is the granddaddy of social media sites. Although it has lost some popularity with teens and young adults, it remains a major workhorse. The great news for marketers is that Facebook has a very balanced audience, with more equal numbers among males and females, and a fairly even distribution among the different age groups. This may be in part because of the age of the site and its general focus. Facebook was around before smartphones, and the focus on linking family and friends is something that appeals to all age groups, including older folks. In fact, 62% of people aged 65+ who are online has a Facebook account.

The bottom line about Facebook is the audience is enormous, and everyone is on there to one degree or another. Facebook has 2.4 billion monthly active users, making it one of the most trafficked websites of all time. Although 1.5 billion people access Facebook periodically using desktop computers, the platform also has a mobile app, and nearly everyone accesses it at least some of the time via the mobile app – including seniors.

Facebook makes it easy to target large audiences. You can do this using organic methods or paid methods or some combination thereof. Facebook not only lets people "connect" and share videos and images, it is also home to a large number of interest groups. People love to form online groups of like-minded people so they can discuss hobbies, sports, academic sites, or access support groups, and Facebook has made it very easy to do it. Rather than going through the hassle of starting your own website, you can leverage the Facebook website to create your own group, and millions upon millions of people do. You can also post messages to reach your customers, and the sharing capabilities of the site will help to automatically get your marketing exposed to larger numbers of people through people's various "friends."

As we will see later, advertising on Facebook is easy, quick, and cheap. You can also laser target advertising on Facebook in ways that have never been possible through the entire history of business.

In our view, no matter what you are marketing and who your target demographic is, you are going to want to be on Facebook.

YouTube

YouTube is nearly as big as Facebook, with some 2 billion monthly active users. It's estimated that some five billion videos are watched on the site every single day. About 73% of adults in the United States use YouTube, with about 60% of monthly active users being male. Nearly all U.S. adults use YouTube, and although there are more males than there are in the general population, it is easy to reach both genders on the site. It is also pretty well distributed among all of the age groups, and those aged 35-55 are the fastest-growing demo. YouTube is fast becoming the go-to source for how-to videos and tutorials, and it's also a place where you can find old music videos, news reports, and old tv shows, and funny cat videos are still quite popular.

The great thing about YouTube is that if you set up your videos the right way, you can get lots of organic views. And even if you can't get organic views, you can use advertising to reach people without spending hardly any money. YouTube is another site that is definitely a must when you are going for social media.

Snapchat

If you are looking to target younger people, the app Snapchat may be of interest. Snapchat is a messaging app that allows people to share images and videos. In recent years, it has become more popular for influencer marketing. However, the app is a little bit awkward, in our opinion, as compared to Facebook, Instagram, and YouTube. At this time, we don't recommend Snapchat for marketing purposes, but it is something to keep in mind as a possibility for the future.

Twitter

Well, everyone knows Twitter. Of course, it probably goes without saying that the site has drawn a lot of attention in part because President Trump uses it – either to great effect if you are a fan or as a menace if you can't stand him. Either way, you have to admit that he can draw a lot of attention using Twitter. Many celebrities are using Twitter to get their message out and to communicate with fans. It has its benefits, and it makes it easy for people to communicate and get short messages across. The site has become extremely political. Although the site is heavily trafficked, compared to some of its colleagues, it's actually on the smaller side. There are reported to be 330 million active users. The site tends heavily male, with some 66% of users being male. Only about 22% of US adults use Twitter, which is quite small compared to Facebook and YouTube. The number of users has declined, and in the 2016 election, and since it became highly politicized. The tweets that people put out have also become easy feeding for news outlets, who often build articles around what people are saying on Twitter.

So how is Twitter as an advertising and marketing platform? Our advice is to stay away from Twitter at the present time for advertising. Reaching people on Twitter with advertising is going to be a more difficult proposition as compared to say Facebook. It is easier for people to ignore ads on Twitter, and although the reach is certainly extensive, it's not very comparable to the heavyweights of social media. However, you can and should use Twitter as a regular user. Just stay focused on one topic and one topic alone. If you need to use it for several topics, create distinct accounts.

Others

There are many other sites that qualify as social media, including Tumblr, LinkedIn, TikTok, and Reddit. However, we just don't think they are worth it. They have smaller audiences, and there is not really anything to be gained by thinking of yet more apps and sites. Consider that if you concentrate on Facebook, Instagram, and YouTube, there isn't going to be a single connected adult that you are not going to reach. And, in our opinion, a business that puts some focus on its marketing efforts, rather than spreading itself thin trying to be at all places at once, is going to have a lot more success.

Why Social Media Marketing Works

There are three main reasons that social media marketing works. The first is the fact that everyone is on social media – of at least one type. Of course, we are exaggerating a little bit. There are probably some older folks who aren't using it, but as we saw above, even most people aged 65+ are on Facebook. The second reason to use social media, is the fact that it does a lot of the work for you. This happens because of the "sharing" capabilities that have been built into these platforms. Sharing allows information to travel around the world at virtually light speed. In the old days, to reach a large number of people, you would have had to spend a fortune to advertise on television, radio, or in national magazines. It would take a long time for your advertisements to go out, provided that you could actually afford it – and sharing would be by word of mouth only, if it happened at all. Someone might tell a friend that they saw a commercial for something interesting on TV, but the friend they told would not *see* the advertisement.

Today, things are completely different. A person who sees a post or advertisement you put up can share it with hundreds of their friends, instantly. This means that although you might pay for a certain number of views or clicks, you're going to get a lot of bonus clicks and views out of it that could increase the number of people who see your advertising by a large margin.

As an aside, we want to talk about magazine advertising a little bit. Of course, that is something that has moved almost completely online these days, but when we first started in the business, if you couldn't afford to get on television, you could use magazine advertising to reach a fair number of people. But what a difference that the world was. First of all, it was expensive. To get a full-page ad in a very modest magazine is something that would cost thousands of dollars. But even worse, it would take weeks to get the ad to run. You would place your order and then wait two months. Hard to believe, isn't it?

And what if the ad didn't work? Then you'd have to tweak it, and submit a new ad, and wait weeks for that ad to run, to see if it did any better. Compare that to Facebook, where you can have an ad reach an international audience within a couple of hours, and if it's not working, you can have a new ad in its place a few hours later. The differences are nearly beyond belief for those of us who were around running businesses in the 1990s.

Back to our discussion, the third major advantage of social media is that advertising on social media is cheap and targeted. In fact, although you could spend millions of advertising on social media if you wanted to, you can also advertise on it and reach a solid number of customers for just a few dollars a day. Social media is not only cheap, but it's easily scalable. And if you want to advertise to Females aged 18-24 living in Los Angeles or both genders aged 54-65 who loved Breaking Bad, you can do both. The targeting capabilities of social media advertising are unmatched.

How to Use Social Media to Generate Profits

The endgame of any business is profits. The key to social media is to use it to start building a relationship with your customer, which is one of the most powerful features that the platform has (maybe we should have mentioned it in the last section), and then leverage that relationship to push your followers into a sales funnel.

One of the biggest factors when it comes to online marketing is trust. This is actually something that goes way back in time. More than a century ago, people were doing mail-order marketing. This was not any different than online marketing, other than the medium used to communicate differently. But consider this. In the late 19th and early 20th centuries, people would get marketing pitches, catalogs, and advertisements in the mail. Now, why would you suddenly cut a check to someone that sent you something in the mail? That idea sounds crazy when you write it down – and yet millions of people did and still do. But one of the factors that is important in that kind of marketing is that the marketer has to build trust and make it seem like you're their personal friend.

As marketing moved online soon after the Internet exploded in the late 1990s, the same principles held. One of the key jobs of an online marketer is to establish trust with prospects. That still holds true today, but one of the advantages of social media marketing is that the medium makes it very easy to build that trust you need in order to get customers willing to give you their money. With social media, you can talk directly to them, rather than just sending them a letter sight unseen. You can post videos of yourself, helping people to see you as a real person. You can take advantage of the two-way communication that social media provides to directly address any concerns people have.

The main goal, however, is to use social media to get fans, people are eager eyeballs who want to see your content. Some of the greatest internet marketers around will tell you that content is king – and that you should give away lots of content. Giving away content will improve your trust factor and also establish credibility. It will help to make you seem like an expert in a given area, and when you establish that, it's very easy to get people to buy from you.

The main thing to look for with social media, however, is the ability to use it as the front end of your traffic funnel. In the pre-social media days, Internet marketers relied on sales funnels and email lists to get people to buy their products. They offered a free product of some kind to do what we've been talking about, establish trust and credibility. In fact, in today's environment, sales funnels and email marketing are very much alive, but you can establish trust and credibility using social media before they even hit your website. This is like putting your trust and credibility on steroids. If someone knows and trusts you from YouTube videos and Facebook posts, when you ask them to visit your site and sign up for your free email newsletter, they are going to do it without hesitation. Social media can help you to dramatically increase your conversion rates at every step in your sales funnel.

Then once they get in the funnel, they are going to be far more ready to buy products, as compared to a lead that just comes across your website.

Going Viral

Of course, "going viral" is one of the great hopes of people on social media. When you create a great post that large numbers of people love, your post can go viral, which means (for the small number of people who don't know) that the post will be shared far and wide by large numbers of people. So, imagine a viewer of your post thinking that her friends definitely need to see this, and so she shares it with 20 people. Then each of those 20 people share it with 20 of their friends…and so on. This is something that wasn't even possible in the old days when people might come across a great advertisement on TV or radio. But today, it is possible to create a massive audience nearly instantly and get your products, ideas, and videos shared across the globe in a matter of minutes. For marketers, this is something that is truly revolutionary.

Formats Used in Social Media Marketing

When you plan on using social media marketing, plan on it being visual. You can always include texts with your posts, but you should focus on getting viewers thoroughly engaged. The fact remains that human beings are visual creatures, and so an image or a video is going to be far more powerful than posting words. In addition, you can always share hyperlinks – to your websites – on social media. This will help you get backlinks as well as getting people to visit your websites.

What Is an Influencer

An influencer is someone who has a large social media following. The following of an influencer is going to trust him or her, which makes the idea of being an influencer a very powerful concept in social media. Many of the fans of an influencer on social media are going to be checking daily to see what the influencer is posting. If the influencer recommends a product or a website, the fan base is going to take that recommendation seriously, and they will at least look at the linked product or website.

There are two reasons influencers are important. The first is that you can pay influencers – often small and reasonable fees – to either put up a post on your behalf, recommend your product, or recommend your website. There are influencers of many different sizes, and so you have a wide range of prices and options to work with. Some influencers may have 10,000 followers, and others might have 150,000 followers, while still others could have millions.

Another reason influencers are important is that you can become a social media influencer in your own right! Becoming an influencer is nothing more than getting a large number of followers. If you are posting daily, this will help you to keep your followers engaged and to keep adding more followers.

How to Find Influencers

The easiest way to find influencers is just to look at the number of followers they have. Alternatively, you can hire an agency to find influencers for you that will post on your behalf for a fee. Some influencers that have relatively large followings but numbers that are not huge might be willing to do trades with you, which can help you get followers of your own without spending money.

Unfortunately, Instagram has made the strange decision to not allow likes to be displayed in the United States any longer. This action may backfire on them, but at the time of writing, it's too early to tell how it's going to work out. This may make it harder to find out who would really benefit you in the influencer game.

This brings us back to Twitter because although we don't generally recommend Twitter, we do recommend it for using influencer marketers. Many celebrities, large and small, have rabid followers on Twitter. And one easy way to drive traffic is to have an influencer on Twitter recommend your product or website. So, don't use Twitter for advertising or to devote a large fraction of your day tweeting, but do consider using it if you can find influencers to pitch your product or website, provided that the audience of the influencer is going to be relevant to your business.

Chapter 2:

Brand Building on Social Media

Building a brand for your business is going to be important for success on social media. It helps bring recognition and recall. In some cases, you can be the brand. This is something many people who train internet marketers do. There are many steps to branding yourself, and we will discuss those and how to integrate them on social media. The most important thing is to be consistent so that you can build recognition across multiple platforms.

Choosing a Name

A name to use for branding is an important first step. If you are an unknown, the brand name should include a short phrase that describes your industry. Internet marketers like Frank Kern can get away with branding his own name because he has been well known for 20 years. But that doesn't necessarily mean you can't brand yourself, but it takes time. Branding yourself will involve repeated postings on multiple social media outlets, and it will probably require a lot of YouTube videos, so that people can see you discussing your niche – which will help to establish yourself as an expert in your niche. Expertise in your niche is what helps with branding.

Alternatively, you can associate with your product. Looking on ClickBank, there are several products aimed and Forex traders. Forex is the foreign exchange where currency is traded. One product is called "Forex Trendy," and they have several customized graphics. If you were promoting Forex Trendy, you could incorporate the name of the product and some of their graphics (which they provide for affiliates) into a brand name. The word Forex is something that is already widely searched, and so that is something that will give you a major leg up in getting found by users.

That is one problem with using just your name as a brand, at a time when you are not well known. Of course, there are ways around this, but going back to the Frank Kern example, his name is something many people are searching for on Google and other sites because he is renowned for giving marketing advice. John Doe, however, isn't as well known if he is known at all – so it will take a long time to get the name John Doe (insert your name here) known as an expert in his niche. But if you incorporate some keywords, then you can leverage the keywords to help build expertise.

So, when you choose a name that you are going to brand, decide if you are going to make yourself the expert that people seek out, or if you are going to make the product something to seek out. As a middle ground, you might hope to brand a company name. This is possible as well, but this faces the same issues as using a personal name in the early stages of your growth. When you create your company name, say it's Acme Services Inc., in the early stages, nobody knows the company name or associates it with your niche. So, a part of your work is going to be associating the name with an important keyword related to your niche, so people begin to build that idea in their head that Acme Services provides expertise on Forex trading, or sells makeup, or whatever business you happen to be in.

Logo Design

Unless you are artistically inclined, we don't recommend designing your own logo. But we definitely recommend having a logo. All companies have a logo; it's another way to get yourself implanted in people's minds and to help them to remember and recognize you. Remember that human beings are visual creatures, and a logo will help implant your brand into their minds. Another way that a logo can help you is that when you are leveraging social media, whether it's YouTube, Instagram, or Facebook, you are going to be posting a lot of images and videos, and including a logo on your media is going to help establish your brand. Also remember that if you are making quality images and videos, people are going to be sharing them with their friends. If you have a professional-looking logo that is on your media, that means every time that you get a share, a new person is going to see your logo, and that helps to expand and establish your brand.

Like we said, unless you are artistically inclined and truly good at graphics design, you shouldn't design your own logo. We also don't recommend using a canned logo from a stock photo site. That might save you money, but if you are serious about building a business, saving money is not something you should have at the top of the list. Think in the long term when it comes to your business. Your logo is going to stay with you for a long time, so you might as well get it done right.

The good news is you don't have to break the bank to get a unique, professionally designed logo. One website we constantly utilize for professionals that can do small tasks for us is Fiverr. If you haven't heard of Fiverr, it's a website you can use to hire independent contractors to do small jobs for you. The original idea was that the job would cost $5, but prices have gone way up as the years have gone by. However, you can find many excellent logo designers that will make a unique and professional looking logo for around $70-100.

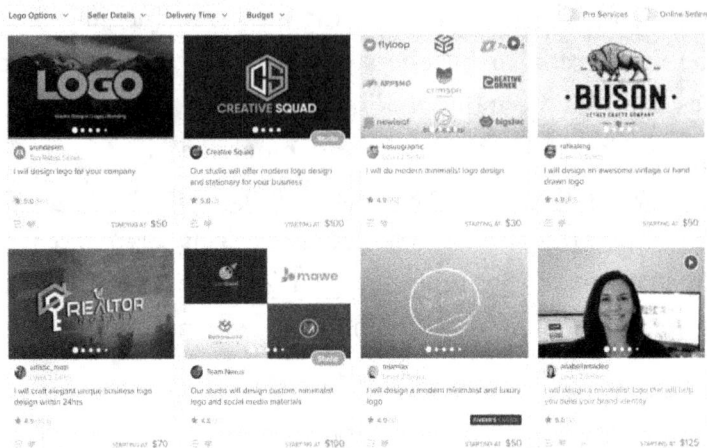

There are a few requirements that you should have for your logo:

- The designer should provide the full-size image that they come up with so that you have it at full resolution. Then you can make copies of it at various sizes that you will need.

- Make sure it has a transparent background. You want to be able to place it on images and on screenshots used on sites like YouTube, where you can create video thumbnails for displays in searches.

- Don't accept mediocrity. Remember, this is something that is going to stay with you and your business for a long time, possibly years, so make sure it gets done right.

- Carefully evaluate past examples that the designer has made. If they don't show many, ask them to send samples. Tell them they can watermark the samples to make it more likely they will share them.

- Read reviews. Fiverr has orders of past reviews, and you will be able to find out if the designer has had past issues with late deliveries or low-quality work.

Colors

Having colors that go together is an important aspect of a logo or any other graphic. There are many guidelines on choosing the right colors that go together. You can just let your designer go with whatever they like, or you can come up with colors on your own and discuss it with them. A good way to get colors that belong together is to use color wheels. There are many websites that have information about choosing colors that blend well; here is an example.

https://brightside.me/article/the-ultimate-color-combinations-cheat-sheet-92405/

A solid, single color is good for branding when it comes to social media. Choose a color that is going to stand out. It can be combined with white, using a color for an image and white for the name of the business.

But remember that you are going to be using your logo on images, which means a single-colored logo isn't always going to work. You might need to have an alternative logo for use on images with a dark background, for example. An easy way to get around this is to have the designer made a colored logo, and then have them make a version of the logo that is solid white for darker images.

Consistency

In order to successfully brand yourself, your business, or your product, it is important to have consistency across all of your platforms. Imagine if Coca-Cola used a different brand name or logo for network television, cable, and YouTube. You would mistakenly think that there were different companies selling soft drinks. The same principle works for you, so you need to settle on a good design and then stick with it. Use the same name and logo on Facebook,

Instagram, Twitter, Pinterest, or any social media platform that you choose to engage with. A unified presence is going to help you build your brand much faster and get the recognition that you need.

Convey a Message or Be Abstract?

When designing a logo, an abstract design is fine, and you are just trying to create a visual image that sticks in people's minds to get them to remember you. However, if you can also convey some kind of message, that can help you increase the value of your logo. The message can be a simple one, and you might want some kind of icon in the logo that will represent the industry that you are in. Or it might be something a little more abstract. If you are a business consultant, you might want to show someone "thinking" to convey the idea that you are going to help your clients with ideas. This is not a critical step, many designers are good at creating abstract images that are memorable, and that is what you are really after with the graphic that is in your logo.

Convey Your Ideal Customer

Knowing who your ideal customer isn't just important for deciding which social media platforms to use and where to advertise, it is also going to be important for your logo designs. Of course, you can go with an abstract design that is simple and has appeal across demographic groups, but if you are specifically targeting one demographic group, that might be important for the design of the logo as well. So, if you are targeting females aged 18-30 or male video game players, you might want completely different logos. Be sure to communicate to the designer who your ideal customer is if you feel that it's important. For some businesses, you might be targeting multiple demographic groups on different platforms, and so you might want variations of your logo by color.

Always Brand Your Posts

To build a brand, always branding your posts is going to be an important step. If you are inconsistent when it comes to branding, then it's not going to be effective. So, you are just going to have to make it a part of your routine to use the name you have settled on and to always include your logo on your posts. The logo doesn't have to be front and center (although it can be at times), you can put it off to the side in a corner. But make sure it's visible as long as it's not interfering with the image. You can also use your logo when creating Facebook pages and so forth to help people identify you and solidify that brand.

Making a Familiar Impression

The point of the logo is to get something that people are going to start seeing all over the place and something that they will associate with and remember. Think about famous logos that you might immediately recall, like Nike, McDonalds, or Amazon. Just seeing the Nike logo by itself will be something that is recognizable. You aren't going to have their reach, but you want that logo and your brand to begin to be implanted in a smaller scale audience, to help breed familiarity. Remember what we discussed in the last chapter; trust is an all-important concept when it comes to online marketing. Branding is one way that you can start to build trust and familiarity. Familiarity by itself is something that is going to increase the trust of your prospects.

Bio

When you sign up for social media platforms, they are going to have a small space where you can enter a bio. Take some time to write a good bio that quickly conveys who you are and what you can do for people. For the purposes of branding, you want to have one bio that you use across all social media platforms. Like the logo, the bio is going to be important for stamping in people's minds some familiarity and is an opportunity to make a connection to the niche of your business. If you have a bio that is different on different social media platforms, this is going to be confusing, and it will work against creating consistent recognition.

One part of your bio is going to be a cover image. In the example below, we show the image used by the company Burt's Bees. Notice that the image has a hashtag that they have associated with their brand. The hashtag conveys a message that they want to incorporate as their company's mission. You should sit down and think about something that is similar. It doesn't have to be a hashtag, but that can be a helpful way to get your brand shared on many social media platforms. But if you don't want to use a hashtag, you can just add a short phrase to your image. If you use a plain image, it might look nice, but by adding the short hashtag, they have turned the image into something that is uniquely theirs while we recommend hiring a professional to get our logo designed when using images for cover photos and so forth using a stock image site is fine.

Notice also that Burt's Bees has consistency. The images below show their home page on Twitter and Facebook, and they have the same logo and the same cover photo, and the hashtag is mentioned in both places. The subtle use of colors is good as well, as subtle seems to work better than loud.

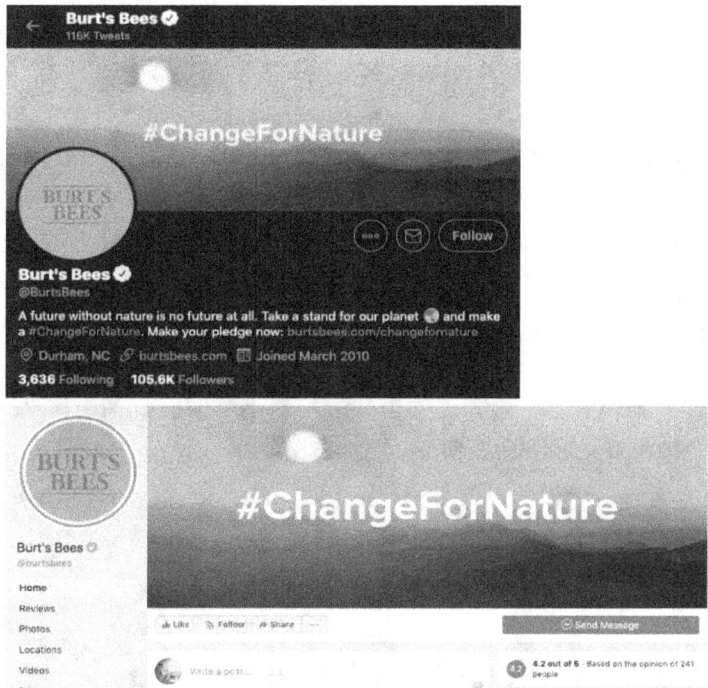

Choose a Branding Font

You might not think about this too much, but any text used in your branding should be consistent as well. Experiment with different fonts in a word processing or image program to see what you like best. You can use Photoshop or a free to download image program like Gimp to play around with making text to use on your cover photo and see which fonts you like best – and which fonts seem to be connected to your brand or product.

Voice and Tone

When you are writing text to help brand yourself, think about the voice that you are going to use in your marketing. This is going to be something that is going to depend on who your customers are. You aren't going to use the same voice with a customer base that is 50+, as you would with a customer base that is 18-24. But no matter what voice you are using, one thing that remains true across all demographics is you want to be sincere and genuine. Try and communicate how you personally relate to your customers. Hopefully, you are promoting a product or service that you would find valuable yourself so that you can put yourself in your customers' shoes and speak to them directly. Try to avoid obscure messages. In your bio, for example, a short sentence that clearly and quickly conveys what your business is about is going to be important.

In a way, showing you the Burt's Bees profile might have been a mistake. Don't misunderstand – it does everything right. But Burt's Bees has been around for a long time, and was already well established before social media platforms were big. So, they can afford to be a little vague.

On Social Media – You Have Seconds

When people are on social media, especially when it comes to mobile apps, their attention span is very short. They are anxious to click or swipe to the next thing, and so you might only hold their attention for a couple of seconds. It's important to set up your logos, cover photos, and your bio to immediately convey what you are offering. While a big, well-known brand like Burt's Bees can afford to wax on about the value of nature without saying what their product is (everyone who is visiting their site already knows what it is, and has probably seen their products in person), they have no idea who you are. So, you have that two seconds to tell them who you are and what you are offering them in the first sentence of your bio. Some social media platforms may be pretty restrictive in the amount of text you can include in your bio, so make sure that your text:

- Is completely clear and worded simply.

- Tells them what you can do for them in the first sentence.

- Speaks in a plain tone that is friendly – don't try telling a joke or use sarcasm.

- Don't try to be profound. When you are beginning the branding process, the point is to communicate clear information about what you can do for your customer, not that you are going to save the planet.

To get some ideas, look up some brands on Instagram, Twitter, or Facebook to see how they have set up their bios – but look for small to mid-range brands. In other words, avoid looking at well-established global powerhouses like Burt's Bees that are not looking to convey who they are (because everyone already knows). Look for smaller companies that are not so well-known to get ideas.

How Serious Is Your Brand?

Some brands need to convey a serious tone. Using emojis in your images or brand logo doesn't help convey seriousness. Are you selling stock market tips? Then you probably don't want to come across as glib or humorous. Interestingly, if you are selling fashion, perfumes, makeup, and the like, you don't want to come across as humorous either. If you are in a niche where there are many big players, study some of the advertising that they are using. Consider that Estee Lauder is not going to be having some guy in the basement, putting up their Instagram posts; they are going to hire professional ad agencies to do it. So, you can learn from what the big brands are doing and mimic it when appropriate. Try and focus on big brands that are the most relevant to your niche.

Consider Multiple Accounts

You aren't restricted to one Instagram account or Facebook page when you are a business. If you have a varied customer base, consider creating multiple accounts on the same social media platforms in order to communicate with each demographic directly. This can be an important part of your branding since you can include sub-niche targeting. If you are selling a product that appeals to 65% females and 35% males, you certainly don't want to leave potential male customers on the table, but the way you communicate with your main customers might not appeal to the males in your audience. So, you can have a sub-branding effort that you could utilize on different social media platforms. You can even use different logos for this purpose if you want to, but keep in mind that you don't want to spread yourself thin when you are trying to launch your business on social media. Consistency in posting on a regular basis and responding to comments by users is going to be an important part of running your presence online. So, make sure that you have the time to spend effectively managing multiple social media accounts before you decide to pursue that path. If you create a sub-branding account but only post to it once every two weeks, then it's not going to add much value to your overall efforts.

Take Stock of Where You Are

Once you settle on your branding, you will need to keep track of your activity and the responsiveness of users to see if it is effective. Testing in the early stages is always good. With that concept in mind, you might not want to settle on a single logo in the beginning. If you are on a budget, it's understandable that you will only have one logo and a branding name. But if you can afford it, you might do some experimentation. See if using different logos changes the level of engagement. Don't be afraid to change logos and brand names early on, if the indications are strong that it's not working. In most cases, however, the branding is going to be secondary to the quality of your posting.

You can even survey people to see what they think is better. Consider setting up an online quiz and paying a mid-level influencer to send traffic to the quiz, where you can show the audience alternative logos for them to vote on.

Actionable Steps

Now that you understand what branding is within the context of social media, it is time to get started with branding your business.

- Start by looking at your audience, or who you think your audience is going to be if you haven't built anything up yet. Determine whether or not you are going to need to split up your social media marketing efforts for different demographics so that you can get a clear picture of whether or not you might need different social media accounts, logos, and cover photos to target different demos.

- Do some research on color palettes to get an idea of the colors you would like to use in combination with your branding. Color is not an all or none issue, remember that you can have the same logo in a variety of colors.

- Think about what wording you want to include on your logo. It should at least include a signature with the name of your company.

- Jump on Fiverr and hire a designer to make your logos.

- When the designer is working on your logo, write a short bio. Make sure the first sentence tells the prospect exactly what you do. After you've made it clear what you offer customers, then you can tell them who you are. Remember that different social media platforms are going to offer different amounts of space for information like bios. But also remember that no matter what, attention spans online are short. So, it's important to be clear and convey as much information as possible in the first line.

- Create a cover photo that will be used across social media platforms. The cover photo can be, but doesn't have to be directly related to your business. Add a short phrase to the cover photo that will help with your branding, as we discussed above. If you are not good at making attractive looking images with text on them – hire your graphic designer for a second job and let them make the cover photo for you. Remember that this is really important, so you want something that looks really good.

- Create your accounts once you have all the images that you need to get started. If you are looking to get feedback on different logos, either run them across friends and family or try and do a survey. If you can't find an influencer to hire, you can run a short ad campaign on Facebook to get a few hundred people to vote on the best logo.

- Keep consistency across your accounts. This is the case even if you have multiple accounts to target different demos. Within each demo, but consistent.

- Maintain a tone of voice for your demo. Remember that you are going to speak differently to people that are different ages, genders, and possibly race or ethnic groups or countries. If your brand is global, you might even have a different social media account for the US and Canada, and Australia or Japan, for example.

Chapter 3:

Elements of a Good Post

Social media platforms are going to vary in the details, but there are some common elements across platforms and some general principles about posting that you should follow. Something that we noted with branding is that it's essential to be consistent. While posting on Twitter or posting on Facebook or Instagram will have their differences, maintaining a consistent persona and brand across all the different social media platforms is something that is going to be important. In this chapter, we are going to discuss some of the elements of a good post that we think you should adopt to get the most out of your social media marketing efforts.

Plan Ahead

Posting on social media is easy. For regular people, that's usually fine. But for a business that is actually a problem. The last thing that you want to do is to post impulsively. When you are using social media in order to promote a business, we advise carefully planning each of your posts. That doesn't mean you have to spend an entire week planning it out, but you should sit down and spend a few minutes to half an hour planning out each post. You can duplicate the post for all the social media platforms, customizing it as necessary but conveying the same message.

First, sit down and decide the reason behind the post. If there is not a reason to post, then you shouldn't post. Of course, you want to be posting frequently, and we do advise posting on a daily basis or at least a few times a week. The fact is, the more you post (to a point), the more rapidly you are going to gain followers. However, posting frivolously is far worse than posting at all.

The important thing to consider here is that you should focus on looking at the post from the perspective of your customer. Your post should have a purpose, and that is to convey the benefit of your product or service to the customer. Alternatively, another valid reason to post is to share information that is of value to your niche, even if you aren't personally providing it. So perhaps you are selling makeup products with your business. Maybe you're having trouble conveying something about your business on a given day, but that doesn't mean you can't post. Find an article with tips that would be relevant for your niche that isn't recommending a specific product, and then share it with a comment on your thoughts about the article. This is a great way to build rapport with your audience, because it conveys the sense that you are sharing a common interest with them, and that you aren't just about selling things. By sharing valuable information without asking anything in return, you can really help to build up trust.

So, planning begins with the reason for your post. When you sit down to plan, write down the purpose of your post in one sentence. Then decide whether you are going to post an image or a video. What message are you going to convey in the media that you present? Start with a clear and concise message. Remember that on Instagram or Pinterest, users are just going to focus on the short text message that is on the image. Keep that in mind as you think about it.

If you are going to make a video, whether it's a long video for YouTube or a 15-second "story" for Instagram, you also need to think about what you are going to convey in the video. We will talk more about this in a bit.

Be Clear and Concise

Whether it's a meme on an image or text that accompanies your social media posts, conveying a simple and clear message is one of the most important aspects of a social media post when you are trying to promote a brand, product, or business. It is better to make your messages clear and to the point, rather than trying to be super clever and mysterious. Remember that big brands have a lot more room when it comes to these types of decisions. We can go back to Burt's Bees social media profile – remember that they are already very well known by their prospects. Even people who haven't used their products have seen their products in many brick and mortar stores. Such a brand like that can afford to focus on flighty and high-minded messages. You can't afford to do that when building a completely brand-new brand. Even if you have a local business that is successful, it's not going to be known across the country or in different countries, so you have to use every interaction as an opportunity to educate the public and let them know what you offer them, and on a secondary level who you are and why they should trust you.

Message Focus

There are a few principles that you can think about when designing your posts that will help you to immediately connect with users. Think about the main point that you want to get across with your post, and then think about 2-3 secondary points that you are hoping to convey. Put these in the outline form.

The first principle is to be specific in what you are trying to say. A fluffy and feel-good message that might make a given Instagram post popular for just sharing around and giving people warm and fuzzy feelings is not going to help you sell products. Don't use any vague language in your posts. Be specific in what you are trying to say so that the reader will have a reason to click through and buy from you at some point. That doesn't mean you should be hard selling in your posts, and you should be working to build credibility and value in your niche.

A second aspect of your message focus should be long-term consistency. Don't give followers the feeling that sometimes someone else is posting, or give them a completely different feel from one post to the next. This is one reason why it is good to have multiple social media accounts if you are going to be targeting different demographics. Try and maintain a solid level of consistency at all times.

Concise is better than long-winded when it comes to social media. Remember the basic facts that we have stated multiple times already – you have just a second or two to grab people's attention. Being concise makes it more likely that you'll be able to pull them in.

Being concise doesn't just mean writing a short sentence, but short sentences are better when posting on social media. It also means using shorter words. Long and complicated words, especially words that people have to pull up a dictionary in order to find out what you are talking about, are not the kinds of words that you want to use in social media, either directly in images or in accompanying text. If you have trouble thinking up short words to use in your posts, jump on thesaurus.com, and look for equivalent words that can convey the same meaning with fewer letters.

Abbreviations and acronyms are also to be avoided. Even some of the most popular abbreviations are not going to be known by everyone, but all of your users are going to speak basic English. Unless you can't completely avoid it, try and avoid using abbreviations in your posts. Only use an acronym if it is very widely known and specific to your niche. For example, if you are selling something to airline pilots, it would be fine to use the FAA.

You might think that if you are marketing to young people, using acronyms and in vogue phrases is acceptable. In a way, it is, but remember that your social media leaves a long-term trail. Five years from now, unless you delete it, your post is still going to be there. Acronyms and phrases used by 18-year-olds today are going to be largely forgotten in a few years. For that reason, it is better to speak in plain English. Young people are still going to get a concise and plainly spoken message that is in plain English, and the benefit of this is that it will solidify your presence on social media over the long term. If you use some catchy phrase that isn't going to be in use a few years from now, your post might become worthless. Remember that as new teenagers get older and get in your demographic, you still want to sell to them, and they might be using totally different lingo than the generation that came just before them. But (hopefully) they will still be speaking English.

Active Voice

Marketers always advise writing in active voice, in preference to what is known as passive voice. When you are using an active voice, you will describe the subject in a sentence as taking action. This can be a little bit confusing to new copywriters, but if you are using an active voice, the subject in the sentence acts on the verb in the sentence. In passive voice, the subject is acted upon. Past-tense words like "was" can be a signal that you are writing in a passive voice. The distinction can be a bit subtle, however, so let's look at a couple of examples.

This is an active voice:

Women love shoes.

Jamie is playing Candy Crush.

John logged into his Facebook account.

The passive voice version of these sentences:

Shoes are loved by most women.

Candy crush was played by Jamie.

Facebook was used by John.

So, remember that passive voice conveys the past to some extent. The subject of the sentence in the passive voice is secondary or coming at the end of the sentence. Active voice is preferred in marketing because it is focused on a definite assertion or action by the subject. Passive voice is a weaker way to state the same message.

Focus on Benefits, Not Features

One of the oldest lessons when it comes to writing marketing copy is to focus on benefits rather than features. Of course, you are going to state your features, but that is a secondary aspect of your marketing efforts. Although you might not think of posting on social media as writing sales copy, you are basically writing a sales copy to promote your business, product, or service on social media. So, start thinking in terms of benefits. New marketers may not be familiar with the distinction between features and benefits, but it's actually an easy concept to understand.

- Benefit: A benefit is the result that the customer gets from using your product or service.

- Feature: A feature is a specific characteristic of your product or service.

Think about a nice umbrella. The features of the umbrella might be the color or the material the handle is made out of . The benefits are being shielded from the hot sun or a rainstorm. "Stay dry even during the worst of times" would be a benefit, "Red color with a mahogany handle" are features. You might want to convey both, but the phrase about keeping out of the rain would be what you place on your image, and if you have a text description that accompanies the image, you can put some of the features in there.

Sometimes it is going to be difficult to think in terms of benefits, but think of someone using the product or service and what it will actually do for them. If you can convey the benefits of using your product or service, this is really going to help drive followers and sharing on social media platforms.

One of the differences between stating features and benefits is that benefits tap into people's emotions, while features tap into people's logic. Emotions are more powerful and fundamental. Again, you are going to want to convey both benefits and features to a customer, but you are going to hook them with benefits, not with features. Features are extra icing on the cake. But in the end, they are going to make a decision to buy largely based on emotion most of the time, and by emphasizing benefits, you can help to ensure that they are going to buy.

Another way to understand the benefit vs. feature dichotomy is that with benefits, you are showing the customer your product or service, even if you are just painting a picture in their minds. With features, you are telling them about it. Showing someone your product is more powerful than telling them about it. And a part of showing someone your product is to get them imagining themselves getting the benefit from it.

An example of a feature would be for a car manufacturer to state that their vehicle got 40 miles a gallon. The benefit would be the money saved from having to buy less gasoline.

When you think of benefits, put yourself in the shoes of your prospect. Think about how your product or service is going to make their life easier, more productive, or help them in some personal way, and then state that to them in your social media messages.

It is important to avoid sounding mechanical in your messaging. One of the best ways to convey benefits is to tell a story about it, and social media platforms are often the perfect way to do it. Think about what a buyer would want to accomplish with your product or service and then show someone getting that benefit in a short video or even a still image. The video stories for Instagram are perfect for this, but remember they are short duration and so conveying the benefit in a short amount of time can be challenging. The flip side of this is that conveying benefits quickly is really going to help your marketing efforts. Imagine that you were selling electric cars. A quick way to show the benefit would be to film yourself, driving the electric car down a country road, or maybe even past a gas station where people are waiting in line to fill up. Then you could use a tagline like "Never have to fill up again."

Think in Terms of Building Relationships

Not every post that you put up should be prodding people to buy something. The primary reason that you are using social media platforms is to build a relationship with your prospects. This is a slow and long-term process, but it will pay off by helping you build a loyal following of customers that will not only buy your products down the road, but they will share your information and recommend your products or services to their friends and associates.

Remember that people don't like the hard sell. The old joke used to be the worst person to be around was the used car salesman, and that is what helped give rise to CarMax, a business that is built around the idea that you are not going to be pressured by a high-pressure salesman. So, avoid doing the hard sell all the time, especially in the beginning. Your first priority should be establishing yourself as a friendly niche expert.

Think about bonding when you are putting up your social media posts. We have to assume that you are going to pick a niche for your business that you know about, which means also knowing the inside language and views of the audience in that niche. If you aren't sure about it, spend some time studying the niche, including following others that are already promoting on the niche to see what kind of insider language and thoughts they are passing back and forth.

Give Away Valuable Information

Any marketing expert is going to tell you that one of the best ways to succeed with marketing is to give away valuable content. This creates value, and it will help you bond with your followers if you show that you are willing to show them expertise and share valuable information without asking anything in return. If you are selling a physical product, you can write articles about using products like it or related products in the same niche. If you are selling an information product, you should share valuable parts of that product for free. For example, if you are selling a video course, if the course has 20 videos, don't hesitate to put snippets of the videos with valuable information up for free. You can even share an entire video. If your content is good, that is one of the best ways to whet people's appetites and get them ready to spend money on the entire course. Think of it as test driving a car. Someone is more likely to buy after test driving a car than they are without test driving the car. Of course, not everyone will be interested and end up buying, but that is beside the point.

Social Media Is Interactive

Remember that social media is a two-way street. This is not like advertising on television or radio where you just throw something out there and then forget about it. Social media is a two-way street, and people are going to be commenting on your posts. You are not necessarily going to have time to interact with all your comments, but you should make it a habit to respond to one or two comments in every post. That makes you open, accessible, and engageable.

In fact, you should go beyond this and actively request conversation with your followers. One way you can do this is to ask a question at the end of the post, and invite readers to respond. For example, say you were selling wine glasses. You could post a picture showing a bottle of red wine and a bottle of white. Then ask:

"Which is better. Red or white? And why?"

Everyone will have their different opinions on this, of course, but the point is it's an open-ended question that is going to get people involved. That will help solidify your brand presence and have people thinking about you – and also thinking about coming back to visit. And notice that we never once mentioned selling wine glasses, rather we avoided selling altogether but focused on something that would of interest to the same people that would be your customers. Asking interesting questions that people might have strong opinions about will also help to get your posts shared.

Start a Blog

Yes, it's a whole new level of extra work – but having a blog can be a great way to leverage your social media. When you have a blog, you don't have to put a huge amount of effort into it, because we are not talking about creating a blog for the sake of becoming a blogger.

Instead, we are going to use our blog in order to have a place where we can put longer and more detailed posts to provide interesting and relevant free content for potential followers. Let's say that you have an idea for seven tips for wearing makeup. You can write this up in a blog post, and then make an image with something like "7 tips for looking your absolute best" on a picture of a woman putting on makeup. Then you link back to your blog. This will help engage readers and get them to follow you since they will be encouraged that you are providing free and valuable content. But remember that if you take this approach, this is not going to be something that you want to do only once or just now, and then, you should do it at least twice a week. Get into the habit of writing a blog post say every Tuesday and Friday and then posting links back to the blog post from the various social media platforms that you are using.

Share News Related to Your Niche

As a part of your effort to convey that you are an expert in your niche, take some time to regularly share news related to the niche. Let your followers know that you are actively engaged with the niche and actively following the latest news related to it. If you go about this the right way, by posting timely and relevant information, for many people, you can become the go-to source for information related to that niche, and this will lead to more followers and later on more people who are buying what you're selling. You will also get more shares if you are posting relevant information on the latest news in the niche.

At times you can just post news and information, but at other times, find ways to integrate the latest news about your niche with the products or services that you are selling. If you can connect your brand with some breaking news about the niche, this can be a powerful way to draw in buyers. But don't force it. Only make a connection if it is natural, and it comes across as honest and sincere.

Post Infographics

An infographic is an image that also includes useful blurbs of text. Of course, make sure that the text included in the image is relevant and useful.

Always Link

No matter what social media platform you are using, always link back to your website. The best place to link back to is a signup form for your sales funnel. Use abbreviated links created by a URL shortener. Include the link with every post and in your bio. Don't throw it in people's faces, but have it there to make a connection available when your posts arouse curiosity. If you are posting something that is a hard sell, then you can say something with the link like "Signup here" or "Click here to buy." If you do not include links back to your main website, you are missing opportunities. When posting on YouTube or Facebook, which allows a lot of text content with your post, you can post multiple links in the same message. In that case, you can include a direct call to action for the link, and you can also post a link to your blog. You should also post links to all of your social media accounts. So, on YouTube, at the end of your video description, put links to your Facebook and Instagram accounts. Also, link back to your blog. Think of this as a signature that you put on every post. Likewise, share a link to your YouTube Channel and Blog on Facebook posts.

Call to Action

A call to action is just a request that the audience does something. In some cases, you are going to directly ask them to purchase your product. This is perfectly fine as long as you are only doing it periodically. If you ask people to purchase something every time that you post, that is going to make you look salesy, and that is going to turn people off. But you need to do it at times. Otherwise, you might not drive any visitors that actually buy.

But there are other types of call to action that you can use on social media. You can use people who see your post to help drive it to a larger audience. Again, you don't want to be a pest here either, but you can ask for help in sharing your message now and then. Ask them to share it with friends and family, and one thing you can do is come up with a hashtag for a post that you can use to get people to share and re-engage.

Later, we will be talking about sales funnels and email lists, and as a part of your business, you are going to want to have a signup from where people can join your email list. An email list is valuable because it's another way to directly join up with and communicate with a group of people that are interested in what you are selling. The email list itself is going to be a more warmed up audience. That is, they are going to be people that are actually interested in buying something. You are going to use social media to drive traffic to the email list, so one call to action should be periodically using is inviting people to sign up to join the list. When you are on social media, you aren't going to necessarily state that you are asking them to join the list to sell to them, you want to tell prospects that you have a free newsletter and that you are going to give them some free information that is going to be valuable to them if they sign up. Remember to keep your promise so that you will maintain credibility.

Mix Things Up

Don't post the same way every single time. First and foremost, mix up your media. That means you should post short videos at times, and post images at others. If you only post single images, it can help, but your profiles are going to be more effective if you post different types of media. You can leverage one social media platform on others. For example, you can post a video to YouTube, and then you can post the YouTube video on Facebook and Twitter. So, you don't have to make a new video specifically for the other platforms. This will also help to get followers from Facebook or Twitter to also follow you on YouTube.

How to Stimulate Curiosity

An effective technique to use in posting is to ask a question. This can either be in a post title or on an image. The question should be designed to get the viewer curious and interested. Going back to the electric car example, even though this isn't really practical it illustrates the point, you could use a question such as "What would it be like never having to buy gas again?"

Use a question to get the wheels turning in people's minds, and do it in a way that is going to make them interested in following you and purchasing your products.

Special Requirements for Different Social Media Networks

Posts on different social media platforms are not all going to be the same, even though you are going to be able to share some commonalities in many cases. If you are posting a single image, that is something you can do on virtually all the platforms. However, there are going to be a few differences.

- On Facebook, you can also include a lot of text. Doing so may or may not be appropriate for a specific post. If you decide to post a lot of text on Facebook, think about ways to make the post relevant to people who are going to read the entire post and also for people that are only going to skim it. One way to do this is to break up the post into sections, with each section making a point that can be summarized with a short, concise sentence. Write down what that summarizing sentence is, and then use it as a bold sub-headline that you can head off the section with. That way, someone who is going to be skimming the post can simply read the headlines to get the gist of it, but those who want the gory details are able to do so also. Facebook actually doesn't have special requirements, and it actually gives you a lot more possibility. You can even post text-only content on Facebook, but remember that while you can do that now and then, you probably don't want to make that the focus, because you want to draw people in with visual imagery and video.

- Of course, YouTube is video only, but you can use images that you are posting on Instagram with your YouTube video or make meme images specifically for YouTube. We will talk more about this later, but YouTube allows you to upload custom thumbnails. This is the image that is going to be displayed when your video shows up in a user search. The purpose of the thumbnail is to attract attention and draw the user in so that they take the time to open your video. In many cases, Instagram images are not going to be appropriate to use on YouTube because a good thumbnail is going to be one that someone can look at and read what the video is about.

- Twitter has a character limit. It was recently expanded from 140 characters, and we believe it is now 210 characters at the present time. That is still a short bit of space, and so if you are going to use Twitter, you will need to convey your message in concise language. But remember that you can post images and videos on Twitter as well. Although users on Twitter are more accustomed to reading text, they are still going to be drawn in by images and videos. Twitter is also a good place to use for simply sharing news items related to your niche, but with your commentary attached. Be sure to use hashtags on Twitter.

- On Instagram, the focus is going to be images and video stories. Short and to the point, with hashtags to help with searches. When you are thinking of posting here, don't bother thinking in terms of text. Your focus should be on the text message that is placed on the image.

- Pinterest is going to be quite similar to Instagram. Focus on the image.

Examples of a Good Post

In this section, we'll look at some examples of good posts that can inspire you. In the first image, we have a bank of America "pin" that was posted on Pinterest.

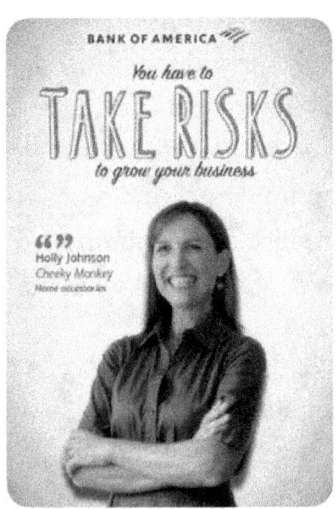

Let's take a look at some of the reasons this is a good post. The first thing is the name of the business, and the logo is prominently displayed at the top of the image, but they are not intrusive. Second, there is a woman in the photograph who is a customer. Why is that important? Remember that we noted most users of Pinterest are female.

Presumably, this is going to help viewers *see the*mselves using Bank of America. The message conveyed in the text is that you are growing your business. When you are analyzing the post, you know that what they are selling is a business loan, but they never state that. Instead, they have listed a benefit – Grow Your Business. A feature would have been "get a loan now with 2% interest". See how much more power you have when stating a benefit? Also note that the woman looks very happy – happy that she is growing her business, and presumably making more money.

Finally, besides the woman in the picture, the most prominent feature of the post is the large text : TAKE RISKS. For entrepreneurs, this is going to speak directly to them. Entrepreneurs see themselves as risk-takers, and they know that in order to build a successful business, some degree of risk-taking – maybe it's just trying to get by without a 9-to-5 job – is a fundamental part of the lifestyle. This is an excellent post because it hits the demographic, it communicates simply and clearly, and it speaks to the niche directly. It also conveys what they are selling but without even stating it.

When you are posting on say Facebook, you are going to want to have a catchy headline to go with the image. So, you might state a benefit in the headline.

Chapter 4:

Daily Actions and Overall Approach

Now you have some idea of what a good post involves. This is something that you should study in detail. Log into the social media platforms that you are interested in and look for posts that have a large number of likes or posts by people with a large number of followers. Then take time to study the different elements that are in the post and how they help with marketing or building a brand. Again, shy away from posts by celebrities or "influencers" that have millions of followers. What they are going might work simply because of their already existing fan base and name recognition. Look for other businesses that are in your niche, or mid-sized influencers to see what they are doing that is engaging followers.

Once you know what to post, the next thing to focus on is how to post. To build a following on social media, you are going to want to get a regular schedule setup. The key to success beyond simply posting good content is to post good content on a regular basis. The more you stick to a schedule, the fast you are going to grow a significant following that will turn into buyers of your product and service. While you can get instant viewers using paid advertising, we recommend building up a little bit of content before you start driving paid traffic. You want people to come to your profile and see that there is something here, rather than just checking out a single post that is unlikely to make them follow you. Also, try and get some family and friends to follow you when you launch your profiles. Social proof is one of the most important concepts in marketing, and if someone sees that you have some followers and likes, it will help to encourage them to give you a follow as well. The sad truth is that nobody wants to be the very first person to follow you even though this is all online. So even if you can only get a handful of friends to follow you and like the first few posts that you put up, it will help to convey the perception that you are engaging, and others are liking your content. This will make new visitors feel more comfortable and willing to do the same. You can also use paid advertising to drive likes, and we will discuss that in a later chapter.

Remember that posting for the sake of posting is not something that you want to get in the habit of doing. So, if you are tired or stressed and can't think of anything useful to say, it is better to just leave posting to another time or even another day. Posting worthless content is not going to help your followers stay engaged or get them to share your content with their friends.

Setting a Posting Schedule

We recommend that you take daily actions on your social media accounts. If you are able to do so, posting 2-3 times per day on Instagram is even better, but it's not essential. You don't want to post too much, and you should only post with a frequency that is compatible with the value that you can offer. Once a day is a good schedule for most people, and one of the ways to make it more feasible is to limit yourself to no more than four social media platforms, and as much as possible, use the same content across different platforms. Remember that if you create a video for YouTube, you can post it to Facebook and Twitter, and if you create an image for Instagram, you can post it to Pinterest, Facebook, and Twitter. So, there is going to be a lot of overlap that is possible between the different social media platforms, and while the overlap may not exact, this means that you can usually design one post and share it on multiple platforms, rather than having to plan out a post for a single platform and do that for each one.

YouTube is one exception to our general rules. The first thing to think about with YouTube is that even if you are only posting short videos with a few minutes of talking, it is going to take more time to plan and execute. The longer your videos, the more prep time you are going to need in order to get them up. With YouTube, a once a week schedule might be sufficient. Remember that you want to provide a lot of value when you are posting YouTube. You aren't going to want to just post of video saying, "Hey, John is here. I'm just hanging out." So, it's acceptable to prepare and wait a few days before posting. Also, remember that your ability to share YouTube videos on some social media platforms may be limited or not available at all. But because of the large audience on YouTube, if you are able to create original video content, it is definitely a must.

Keep in mind that you don't have to start off with a set rule. For social media posting to be effective, it must be frequent and regular. There is a lower limit beyond which you are going to be slowing your impact to the point where it's not worth doing. In our opinion, posting once or twice a week is far too infrequent. It will take a very long time to get a following that way, and posting infrequently is not going to keep your following engaged. At least three times a week is a minimum for posting to Facebook, Twitter, and Instagram. It is better to post daily on those platforms. On Twitter, posting a few times a day, as long as it's relevant, is even better. Of course, posting on Twitter can be easy, and you can leverage your other posts, so take an image from Instagram and post it on Twitter too. Again, YouTube is the exception, and less frequent posting is acceptable.

Prep Time

Begin your day with a 20-30-minute time frame that is used for prep. State the goal of your post and come up with a concise and engaging statement that can be used as a headline. Then decide which platforms to post on. Since it is fair use to put anything you develop for other social media platforms on Facebook, we recommend thinking of Instagram or YouTube first, and then posting the content used for that on Facebook and Twitter. You can then elaborate if you feel it is helpful since you can post extra text on both platforms.

Also, have a standard signature that you use, which will have backlinks to your sales page or email landing page, your blog, and your other social media sites.

Engagement

Check up on your accounts 2-3 times per day in order to engage with followers. It is important to keep engaged with them and respond to comments and questions in a timely manner. Each time that you put up a post, be the first person to comment. This can help drive conversation and let users know that you are a real person who is willing to talk to them in the comment section. You don't have to make social media your life, but if you put some effort into engagement, the more productive your efforts on social media are going to be. Generally, we recommend posting one comment yourself and then reacting to 2-3 comments that other people post.

Don't Be Discouraged

In the beginning, you are not going to get much attention on social media. It takes time to build up a good following and have an active user base. So, you might feel like you are all alone in the world in the early part of your social media marketing career, but don't get discouraged. Over time, you will build up a following as long as you are putting up relevant and valuable posts. Persistence is going to be the key to success over the long run, and those who are able to push through the early stages, which are not going to seem like they are productive are going to be the ones who succeed in the end.

Leveraging the Followers of Others

There are many things that you can do in order to increase your followers across networks that don't involve spending money. The first thing is to put a link to one of your posts – when it's relevant. In other words, go on the feeds of other people in your niche and when there are posts that you can contribute to, leave a meaningful comment and leave a link back to one of your posts. The important thing in regards to this approach is that you avoid being spammy, and you use the technique sparingly. You don't want to come across as someone who is desperate to drive traffic back to their own posts, so only do it when it is directly relevant.

One way to make sure that you can do it when it's directly relevant is to look at other people's feeds for content that you can post about, too, with your own unique spin on it. When you find something, then put up a post on your own feed, and then return to the original post and figure out a way to relate it back to what you posted.

A good way to do this that seems less intrusive is to link across platforms. So, let's say that you put up a YouTube video on a given topic in your niche. Then you can jump on Facebook and Twitter and look for people that are discussing the topic, and then make a comment, and suggest that they check out your YouTube video. You can also use this method outside traditional social media, posting in blogs and forums. The only thing to keep in mind about blogs and forums is many of them have rules about trying to sell things, especially affiliate marketing products; in other words, that is prohibited. But if you have content that is purely informational in character, such as a helpful YouTube video, it should be OK to post it in most places.

Leverage Quora

An interesting website to leverage in an effort to get followers is Quora. If you are not familiar with it, this is a question and answer website. People post questions on Quora about virtually any topic, and you can answer questions and include links back to your posts. The only thing about Quora is they don't like spamming, and so you should take the time to only post there if you can provide a detailed and thoughtful answer to questions about your niche that people are posting. One thing you should never do on Quora is posting a direct link to an affiliate marketing product or a sales page, even if it's your own sales page. But what you can do is post links to relevant social media posts where you can add more value. For example, if your expertise was plumbing, you could post a video on YouTube where you show how to fix a leaky bathroom faucet. Then find questions about this on Quora, and post a verbal explanation about the process in response to the question, with a link back to your YouTube video.

Avoid spamming even if you have something relevant to say. So, don't open up Quora and post a link to your video in response to ten different questions over the course of an hour. Just post it once and then find some other reason to answer a question. The backlinks will help to drive your content, and people seeing it on Quora may be interested in checking out your video.

Chapter 5:

Instagram

In this chapter, we are going to specifically address the topic of using Instagram as one of your primary social media platforms. This is a great platform to use, but there are some caveats. The main thing to consider when using Instagram is that the audience is going to tend younger. That doesn't mean that it is exclusively a younger audience, but if you are marketing something that is relevant to senior citizens, this is not where you want to be spending your efforts. If you have something targeted at young adults, this is definitely the place where you want to be. If you are marketing something that is sufficiently general that any adult is going to have potential interest, then Instagram can be a part of your overall social media marketing strategy.

Another factor to consider when using Instagram is to ask yourself if the product or service that you are offering is suitable for the platform that Instagram offers. Although they have recently allowed posting of video, the videos that you can post on Instagram, so-called "stories," are only 15 seconds long. Second, despite adding video content, it remains primarily an image sharing site.

Of course, that still leaves the door open as a marketing platform. In the old days, advertising in magazines was a powerful way to pull in customers. Many advertisements in magazines are full-page photo ads. So, in a way, magazine ads were the Instagram of their day. Although it might not be immediately obvious, start thinking about ways that you can promote your product or service using a photograph and brief message and drive traffic back to your website.

Good Photographs

The first thing that is required for marketing on Instagram is a good photograph. This might put you off. Do you need to have a photograph that you personally take? The answer is no. So, it would be a good idea to sign up on a stock photo site where you can get a large number of downloads per month so that you will have access to some professional photographs that can be used at least in part with your Instagram campaigns. If the photograph looks good, the message conveyed with it is going to be more important than whether or not the photograph is yours or one from a stock image site.

We advise study before taking action, so that you can get the most out of your efforts. So, take some time to learn your way around Instagram. First of all, create an account. It is possible to have linked accounts with Facebook since they own the app.

Then browse around to find images that are related to your niche. Study the images that look the best to find the elements of a good Instagram posting. Of course, we never advise directly copying someone, but a bit of mimicry, especially when you are first getting started, is not going to hurt. The basic rule is finding out what is already working and do exactly what they are doing.

There are two ways that you can post. You can post a plain image, or you can post an image with an overlaid text. As a marketer, you are probably going to want to include some text along with your logo (but don't make the logo prominent). You can create the image with text as you go, or you can make it ahead of time.

You can also add some text to your posting. This is not going to be an extensive amount of text, so you need to learn to get straight and to the point when you write text to accompany your posts.

Simultaneous Posting

One of the nice things about the Instagram app is that you can use it for simultaneous posting to Facebook, and you can also share on Twitter. So, if you have a good image that is ready to go, this will help you save time.

Posting Procedure

The procedure for posting on Instagram is quite simple.

- Prepare your image ahead of time. As a marketer, you aren't going to want to post impulsively and should have everything planned out. Think about the benefit you want to convey, how that benefit is going to be expressed in the image and what text you want to use to convey your message, and the text caption to include with the photo.

- Instagram allows hashtags to help with search when people are looking for topics related to your image. Write down a list of 8-12 hashtags to use before you go ahead with the post (we want to avoid thinking on the fly, so that is why we advise doing it now).

- Open the Instagram app and click the + button. Select the image from your camera roll (be sure to save it to your camera roll before beginning this process).

- If desired, you can run the image through one of their filters.

- The final step is to add your caption and hashtags. You can also opt for Facebook posting here as well, and other options like setting the location.

We advise that you make your profile more interesting by mixing up media. You are going to have to put either a video or an image when you post to Instagram, so you are not going to be able to post text only. However, you can post abstract images with text on them, or even create a solid black or white background and put text and a logo on it. In any case, you should post videos on Instagram periodically in order to make it more interesting.

Helper Apps for Instagram

There are many apps that can help you prepare your Instagram posts. Some of them will help you add text if you want to or make other adjustments that you find necessary. They can allow you to post directly to the app or save to your photo library, and then you can open Instagram to post directly.

You can also find apps that help you create video stories for Instagram. Helper applications for this purpose are also available online for a price. It can be worth making a small investment for these tools, since they can help you make your videos look professional, and they will be perfectly formatted for posting to Instagram.

Posting Frequency

In order to build a following, we recommend that you post 2-3 times per day. Posting on Instagram is something that is going to take a little more effort because a little more frequency of posting is best for this site. The good news is that posting on Instagram is pretty easy, so it's not going to be too time-consuming overall.

Your Link

One of the most important things with Instagram is your profile. The profile allows you to enter a short bio – and most importantly, you can put a link there back to your website. We recommend that you build an email landing page that is directly related to the sales of your product, and that you use this link as your website link on your Instagram profile. This will help to drive traffic to your main website as you start to build up a significant Instagram following.

Second, be sure to add a good profile picture. However, we advise using your logo as your profile picture. Remember, this is about branding and promoting your business, not you personally. There is one exception to this, if you are going to be building a business brand around yourself as some kind of niche expert or coach, it may be appropriate to use your own image as a profile picture.

It is also allowed to include an email address, so you can include an email address that you want to use for business purposes here. Just be sure to answer relevant inquiries that you might receive (and take that as an opportunity to send people a link to your email landing page). This is an example of an Instagram profile. Notice that their link is found just below the bio (right above the Follow, Message, and Email Buttons):

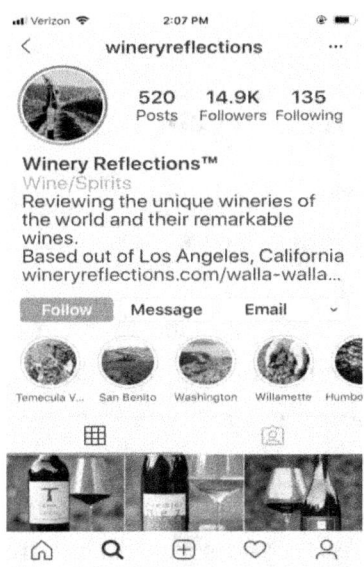

When we click the link, it does what we just advised – it opens up a signup form:

That isn't necessarily the best landing page in our opinion -but the function is perfect, and this illustrates how you should set up your

Instagram profile.

Instagram Business Accounts

If possible, we recommend keeping the personal and the business aspects of your life separate. There might even be legal reasons to do this, but there are many practical reasons as well. Instagram allows you to create business accounts, and this can include niche-specific Instagram accounts. You should utilize this to help you drive your business. At the time of writing you can create up to three niche accounts with a business, and so this can be a way for you to post to Instagram targeting specific niche market segments, or if you are offering different products and services that are not directly related, you can use the different accounts to promote each individual niche.

First Step: Build Up Some Content

Yes, this process is going to take some patience, but it will pay off for those that follow it. In the following sections, we are going to talk about some ways that you can leverage other Instagram accounts to help drive traffic, but before you do that, you want to establish your own presence on the platform.

So, this is going to involve posting frequently with good content for a period of time. Again, we recommend that you post 2-3 times per day on average. Before you approach anyone else or use paid advertising, our advice is to follow this procedure for a month. That way, when you go and approach another Instagram account, you will look substantial as, by that time, you will have somewhere between 60-100 posts. You want to look like you have something of interest that will benefit the followers of other Instagram accounts so that you can offer to make trades. People who see that you only have 2-3 posts are not going to be interested in dealing with you.

We also recommend a warm-up time to build up the number of your posts even when using paid advertising. That way, when people go to your account as a result of your paid advertising, they are going to see that you have substantial and interesting content already, and they are likely to give you a follow and perhaps like and share some of your posts. Again, aim for some variety. Video doesn't have to be a major component of your posting, but after the first month, you should aim to have about 3-4 video stories on your profile as well. If your profile has some content and it's more interesting, people are going to be more likely to visit the link on your profile and even sign up on your email list.

Trading Posts

After you have gone through phase one of your Instagram life, the time is right to start making an effort to drive traffic. The first trick to use in order to gain some traffic and more followers is to seek out small and mid-sized Instagram accounts that have between 10,000 and 50,000 followers. Then you are going to ask them to promote your account in exchange for you promoting theirs.

Every Instagram account has a direct message button and email address on the profile page. Try direct mail on Instagram first to contact them. If they don't respond, send an email (some accounts might not read their Instagram messages). If they don't respond after sending the email, don't pester them and move on to another account instead.

Since you have a new account, you are going to have to offer them a little more than what they are giving you. A typical arrangement is that an influencer account will offer you a post on their account for a certain amount of time, or they will recommend to their own followers that they follow your account, again for a certain amount of time.

One approach you can take is to ask them to put up a post for say 12 hours or a day, and in exchange, you will put up a post directing people to their Instagram account for 3-5 days. That doesn't sound fair, but in truth, it is fair if they have 10,000 followers, and you only have 100.

Before taking this approach, you might want to run some paid advertising so that you can get some more followers on your own, and make the offer a little more attractive.

You can make this offer to several different Instagram accounts. Don't do more than one at a time, but try to do one a week. See what the results are, if you are able to build up a lot of followers and you can keep finding people that are willing to post and recommend a follow, this procedure can keep working for you.

Paid Posting

One of the interesting things about Instagram is that you can basically do paid promotion without any involvement of Instagram at all. The way to do this is to approach an account with a larger following, direct message them and ask them if they accept paid postings. Of course, everyone likes to make a buck, and many influencers on Instagram make their money this way. So, it shouldn't be too hard to find Instagram accounts that are willing to promote your account for a price.

The amount of money required is going to depend on the size of the account. You don't have to go for the gold and try getting paid promotions with the largest accounts, but expect to pay more for someone that has a million followers versus someone that has 50,000 followers.

When you contact them, ask them what their fees are in order to make this kind of arrangement. In addition to a flat fee for posting on your behalf or recommending that their users follow you, they may have a scaling price depending on the amount of time the post is left up. For smaller accounts that might have 50,000 up to 250,000 followers, they might charge you anywhere from $35-$200 to leave your post up for 12 hours or 24 hours. People set their own rates, so we can't give you exact amounts that are going to be charged for large Instagram accounts in your niche, so you are going to have to start contacting people in order to find out what it's going to end up costing.

You can also try contacting people to directly promote your product or service, if you are confident in it. They might want to get a free sample, or you can shoot them a video demonstrating the product. If you make games or apps, Instagram influencers can be a great way to get some direct traffic, if they recommend the app on their profile.

Be Ready for Traffic

Later in the book, we are going to talk about landing pages and having an email marketing list. Before you do anything, you should have that setup. The point is that you have to be ready to leverage any traffic that might come your way and capture leads. Otherwise, you are wasting your time. When a large Instagram account is driving traffic to you, people are going to be checking out your profile, and some of them are likely to click on your website link. So that is something you are going to have to set up before you use Instagram for promotional purposes. While the main reason that you are going to be paying people for exposure is to get followers to build a long-term relationship with on the social media platform, and so you aren't necessarily expecting immediate signups or sales, you should be ready in case some people are willing to sign up or even buy your products.

Summary

Instagram is a great app, and the nicest thing about it is, provided you can get or take engaging photographs and write great captions or put great text on your images is that it's easy to use. Posting frequently on Instagram is not something that generally takes a huge amount of effort, and the platform makes it easy to link back to your site. The second advantage of Instagram is the ability to directly contact influencers that already have large followings and get them to promote you or even your products.

Chapter 6:

Facebook

Facebook remains one of the most powerful social media marketing tools that are available. Even if it is not your primary platform for promotion, it can be leveraged to get more reach, and one of the most powerful tools that we are going to consider in chapter 8, Facebook advertising, is the best reason to have a presence on the site. You can also use Facebook advertising to run the same ad on Instagram. That is actually a good way to test to see if your products are relevant for the Instagram audience without putting in the effort to build an Instagram profile. You can run ads on the platform through Facebook and see what kind of response they get. If you find that you aren't getting many clicks or reactions, then that would be telling you that Instagram is not an ideal social media platform for your product or service.

Setting up a Business on Facebook

You must have a personal profile on Facebook, but you should search Facebook for business and set up a business account on top of it. It is a fairly easy and straightforward thing to do. This is going to be something you'll want to do for the purposes of advertising. Even if you are not going to advertise on Facebook right away, you are going to want to have this step-in place.

Creating a Facebook Page

For a direct presence on Facebook, creating a Facebook page for your business is going to be the way that you promote your business on Facebook. A Facebook page is associated with your personal

Facebook account; however, the association is not direct or public. People will only know about it if you invite them to the page. Whether you invite friends or family to the page is going to be entirely up to you. But for those that are concerned about privacy and keeping the business postings on Facebook separate and distinct from your personal profile, it will do exactly that for you.

The first step is to jump on Facebook and select pages. It will then allow you to visit Facebook pages that you have created, or you will be able to make a new page. When you create a new page, the first thing that you will do is to create a name for your page.

As we stated earlier, our advice is to have a uniform presence across platforms for your business. And so that means if you have created an Instagram page for Acme Wineries, you should name your Facebook page Acme Wineries as well. Also, use the same logo and cover photo across your platforms.

Facebook is going to ask you for your profile photo to put on the Facebook page. Here, you want to use your business logo. Then it will ask you to add a cover photo.

About Page

Next, you will probably want to go to your About page. The About page allows you to enter general information about your business, including phone number, address, and so on. You can also add a mission statement and fill out "Our Story," which is basically a spot where you put a bio for the business. Facebook is a lot more extensive than other social media platforms, so you can be far more descriptive with text when filling out this information. The Our Story section can have a cover photo, headline, and text. If relevant, you can also add team members to this section.

Facebook Page Button

On the main Facebook page, you are going to notice that just below the cover photo, there is a section that says, "Add Button." Don't ignore it! This is a chance to put a call to action button to take visitors to your Facebook page to your website. You can use it to direct users to a shop or to sign up for your email newsletter.

Posting

After you have everything set up, you can start posting. Our recommended frequency for posting on a Facebook page is 3-5 times per week up to daily. Keep our admonition in mind, however. If you don't have something worthwhile to say on Facebook, just let it go until something comes to mind. Facebook is more content-intensive, and so you should be sure to add value to your postings.

Think of posting on a Facebook page as a Facebook account for the business. We discussed posting earlier, and you should follow the advice in that chapter, but the basic idea here is that you are going to be posting on the business page in the way that you would post on your own Facebook profile. But the key is to keep things relevant and informative. Don't post anything frivolous on a business page.

One of the reasons for having a Facebook page is to tie things together. So, when you post a YouTube video, post it on your Facebook page as well. When you post a photogram on Instagram, also post it on your Facebook page. If desired, you can do that directly from Instagram, but we actually recommend using the same image but posting directly to the page and adding some more text content.

From time to time, you can also use it as a place to post simple text. The point is to make it useful and engaging for any visitors that come across the page. The longer your feed is, the more time they are going to spend on the page, and the more likely they are to follow you and share your posts.

Tying together a blog – assuming you have one – is also something that you want to use Facebook for. Each time that you post to your blog, grab the link to the post and then post that on your Facebook feed.

Advertising

We are going to be talking about advertising on Facebook in chapter 8. So, we aren't going to go into the details here. But the main way that we prefer to use Facebook is for paid advertising. In our view, the Facebook page is secondary, and we will use it to help give some extra exposure to our other sides and social media accounts.

Chapter 7:

YouTube

Making videos isn't a requirement, but we highly recommend it. Video is one of the most engaging ways to interact with people using social media, and YouTube is one of the most massively trafficked websites on the planet. If you get good at making videos, you can use it to demonstrate expertise in your niche or to demonstrate products that you are selling. You can integrate it with any kind of business. If you have a Shopify store, you can use videos on YouTube to showcase your products, and then link directly back to the product on the store. You can also use YouTube to demonstrate expertise in a subject area if you are selling information products or affiliate products. They also let you post affiliate links with your videos, unlike some other sites.

The good news is that you only have to be decent at making videos, you don't have to be the best person, have the best voice, or be the most photogenic. The approach that works the best with YouTube videos is to be natural and relaxed. Another good thing about it is you don't have to worry about not being so good at first. Remember that everyone starts somewhere. Second, you will get better with time, provided that you make videos on a regular basis.

Posting Frequency

YouTube production is a little more involved than posting on other sites, and so it's not necessary to be posting daily. In fact, that might even harm you if you are not able to put the time in to make a quality video on a daily basis. If you can post good videos daily, and some people will find that it comes more naturally to them, that is fine. But if you can't, don't worry about it. Our recommendation to build a following on YouTube is to post between 1-3 times per week.

The amount of production involved in making your video is going to, in part, determine how frequently you can post. Some people simply set up a webcam or use their mobile phone and talk to the camera. If you can do that effectively and your videos are not very long, you'll be able to post more often.

Video Length

The most important thing in a video is engaging content that provides useful information. A video doesn't have to be an hour long. It can be as short as 3-5 minutes, if people get something useful out of it. Of course, the shorter videos are more likely to be viewed all the way through the end, but remember that you are using YouTube as a tool, and not necessarily as an end in itself. So, you want your content to be significant enough so that people are going to check the links that you place in the video description and visit your main website.

There are not any firm rules, but unless you have something really compelling to discuss or you are offering some sort of video course or coaching, and you want to post samples, you don't want your videos any longer than 15-30 minutes or so. The short attention span of online users is a factor on YouTube, as well. It may be the case that the information you have to offer is so useful, and your presentation is engaging enough to keep people on your video that long, but people are always anxious to move on to the next thing when they are online. In many cases, a five to seven-minute video is going to be appropriate.

Follow Examples

Before you start making videos, look at what other people in your niche are doing. This is another example of finding the expert and do exactly what they are doing with your own spin on it. So, research your niche on YouTube, first to see if people are getting significant numbers of views to make sure that there is an audience for you on the site. More than likely, there will be because quite frankly, everyone is on YouTube at least some of the time.

The second thing you want to look for is what kind of content are they offering, and how are they offering it. You will want to make videos that are a similar format if they are getting a large number of views. You can also make videos on similar topics. Of course, once again, you don't want to copy anyone, but you should certainly use inspiration and use what already works.

Something that we strongly advise is that you get a free plugin for your web browser that is called vidIQ. This handy plugin will help you spy on the competition. One of the things that it does is it pulls out the keywords that are used as tags by a given video. If you are able to see what keywords videos in your niche are using to drive a lot of traffic, then you will know to use some or all of these keywords on your videos as well.

Also, look at the title and description of popular videos. Pay special attention to how they set up their title, as this is one of the most important parts of the video.

The Thumbnail Image

The thumbnail image is often an afterthought when people upload YouTube videos. Of course, that isn't the case for experience YouTubers that have a large number of views, but new users might not be thinking too much about it. But you do need to think about it … it is one of the most important parts of your video. The reason is that when people are searching, they are going to be glancing at thumbnail images that the site displays in searches like this:

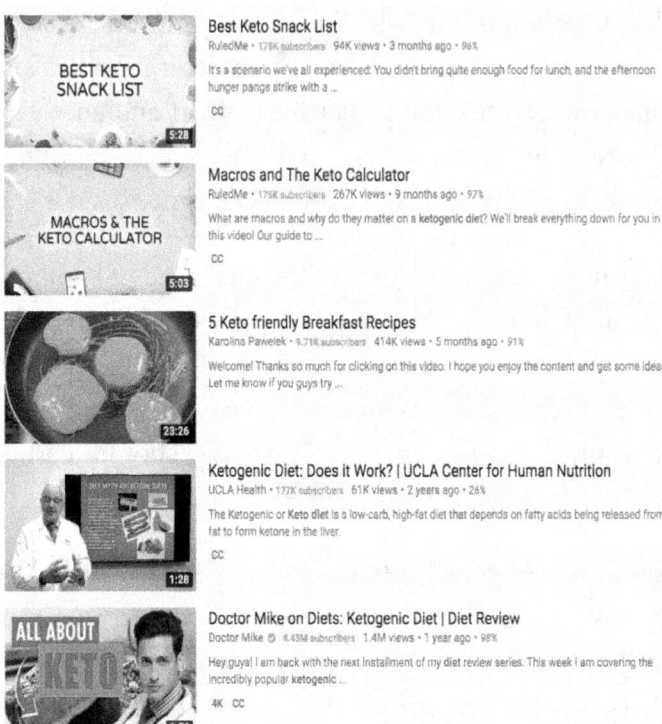

In this search, we used the phrase "keto diet." Notice the top two videos, they have the title of the video in the center of the image, against a background that makes the title stand out. This is a great way to draw attention to the video and to get people who are searching on the relevant topic to go ahead and click on it.

At the bottom, we also see a common method that is used. The person that uploaded that video has put a picture of themselves, along with the word KETO against a yellow background to make it really stand out. As you notice, it has 1.4 million views. The video just above it is from UCLA medical center, but it only has 61,000 views. There are many factors at play, of course, but the thumbnail is one thing that is going to help draw views because the video at the bottom simply stands out more, and it makes it clear that the video is about the topic that we searched for.

The video above the UCLA video has a horrible thumbnail – but the title of the video is an excellent title. The title is specific, and it is a phrase that people probably search for directly. While that video has had quite a bit of success, probably due to the very relevant title (and the owner of the channel may have a large number of subscribers), we believe it could have even more success if it had added some clear text like the bottom video in the image.

Here are some more examples of thumbnails. In this case, we searched for "make $100 a day".

Notice that these videos have clear text and imagery that will draw someone who is looking for information about making money. The first image at the top is probably the best because the solid orange background and readable text immediately makes it clear what the video is about. You don't even have to read the title of the video, because he has the title in the image. The last two images are also good too. These are examples that are not using the title, but rather the visual imagery of a $100 bill – together with a phrase that is pack with meaning. By saying copy and paste, they are telling you that in the video, they are going to show you the exact steps you need in order to make $100 a day.

Setting Up Your Video

Besides the thumbnail, you are going to want to think about keywords when making your video. Let's look at the last video in our second list of thumbnails. First, we can use Vid IQ to pull up the keywords that he used for the video.

This guy really knows what he is doing, notice that he ranks for almost every keyword. In fact, the video had more than 19,000 views after only being posted for two days.

Notice that he is using many long-tail keywords. If you are not familiar with long-tail keywords or using Google Keyword Planner, these are topics that you should become familiar with before getting your YouTube channel started. Remember that YouTube shows up in Google searches, and so you are going to want to choose keywords that people are searching for so that you can leverage the power of the YouTube site to show up in regular search engine results.

His title is also very good.

> Make $100 Per Day For FREE To COPY and PASTE! (Earn Money Online)

The thing to notice about the title is that he has the main phrase that he is targeting, which is "Make $100 Per Day". Second, he used the word FREE, which is something that is going to pull people in, because a lot of people are always searching for free advice. This is followed by the phrase used in his thumbnail, COPY, and PASTE, which tells the viewer that he is going to show them the exact method they need to use in order to make $100 a day (we leave it for the reader to decide whether or not his method is valid). Finally, he has used another relevant key phrase in the title, which is "Earn Money Online."

Now let's look at his description. The first thing that we want to examine is how the description is setup. Notice that he has put links both at the top and at the bottom of the description. A lot of YouTubers put their links at the bottom of the description, but this is a mistake, because many people who view the video aren't even going to open the description, much less scroll all the way to the bottom even if they do.

> Let's make money online! This method can make you $100 a day!
> My Top 2 Methods...
> 📥 Full eCom Training + Mentorship 👉 https://ecomelites.com
> 📥 Full Affiliate Training + Mentorship 👉 https://savageaffiliates.com
>
> Message me here for template: https://franklin.live/FreeNow
>
> 🔔 Subscribe to Frank! https://franklin.live/Subscribe
> 📸 Follow Frank! https://franklin.live/Instagram
> 🛒 Best Online Deals! https://franklin.live/BestDeals
>
> This is an awesome to way get started online for beginners! Its literally copy and paste and the best way to make money online in 2019.
>
> The first step is to go to a website called CB Engine. On this website you can from products that you can promote and earn online with. This is called affiliate marketing and its a great way to start online.
>
> Then you want to go to clickbank.com and sign up s you can get your affiliate link. You can use these links to make good money online. Make sure you promote products that are hot in the industry.
>
> When you want to make money online it's important to watch these tutorial videos all the way through. The next thing I do after signing up to Clickbank is I then go and find blogs online. Once I find the blogs I leave a comment in the comment section and leave my affiliate link in there. When someone clicks the like I will be paid just by working at home!
>
> This is a great way to work from home is to start doing affiliate marketing. Making money using this method is the best for beginners! You can do it for free, don't need a website and can do it from anywhere in the world!
>
> The best way to make money online and passive income from the internet is by watching this video all that way to the end. I give away some free content to help you scale this to the next level!
>
> 📥 ACCESS YOUR FREE TRAINING VIDEOS! 📥
> FREE Ecom Training! https://franklin.live/Ecom
> FREE Affiliate Training! https://franklin.live/Affiliate

Now notice the text in the description. He is focusing on the keyword "Make Money Online," which is also used in his tags. Google will index the YouTube video, so put your main keyword in the description that goes with the video at least three times, but no more than five times. He also throws in 2019 in several places, so that he can simultaneously target Make Money Online 2019.

Another key phrase he has included in the description text is affiliate marketing. That also appears twice in the text. The word ClickBank is also present, which is a website for affiliate marketers, and so people searching for affiliate marketing may also be searching for ClickBank.

Promoting Your Video on Other Sites

After you have uploaded your video, you want to make some effort at organic promotion. The first way to do this is to post it on your

Facebook page. When you do that, put a link in the description that takes people back to the YouTube page. Next, you will want to post it on Twitter. Also, create a blog post that goes with the video. If you write a transcript for your video, then put this text in the blog post with the video at the top of the page. Having the text in there will help get your blog post indexed by the search engines. You can also promote your video on other social media platforms and using it in answers you put up on Quora and in online forums.

Earning Money from YouTube

YouTube allows people to earn money with ads on their video channels. You have to become eligible for it and request it, but this is pretty easy. By adding advertisements to your videos, you can earn some extra money. And if you grow to the point where you are able to get millions of views, you can actually earn substantial money just from the advertisements on your YouTube videos alone.

Chapter 8:

Advertising on Facebook and YouTube

Now that we have learned how to set up a Facebook page and post videos on YouTube, it's time to talk about advertising. The fact is advertising with Facebook and YouTube is one of the best ways to do paid advertising that there has ever been. It is a very low-cost relative to other paid advertising methods, and it is also easy to set up and effective. There are a lot of people around who are going to give you negative spin about doing paid advertising, but quite frankly, we can't see doing without it in today's environment.

Facebook Advertising

The great power that comes with advertising on these sites is in the number of people you can reach for low-cost advertising, and the level of direct control and targeting that is available. We will start with Facebook advertising, which also covers Instagram advertising. The two are actually launched in the same campaigns by default, although you can choose to keep them distinct if that is your preference.

Audience Insights

The first thing to do when you are preparing to do Facebook advertising is to do some studying when it comes to the audience. Facebook gives you all the tools that you need in order to do this. You need to open up the Facebook advertising manager and go to the Audience Insights page.

The Facebook Audience Insights page lets you investigate audiences to see how large they are, look at their demographics, including gender, age, location, job title, and so forth, and most importantly, filter down by page likes. You will see that the page has an INTERESTS tab; this is where you want to focus in order to drill down your audience to find people who are interested in your niche.

One of the methods we use is that we find large competitors in our niche that are likely to have Facebook pages. This will enable us to target people that are already interested in the niche. It doesn't bother us that they have already bought from a competitor. Did the existence of McDonalds stop Burger King and Wendy's? In fact, it did the opposite – it encouraged them. So rather than fearing our competition, we choose to take advantage of players in our market.

So, when Facebook is asking you for interests when creating an audience, you can start by putting in the names of products or companies that are in the same niche. If you are selling organic food, then you are going to want to target people on Facebook who have liked the Whole Foods Facebook page. They are already interested in organic food (more than likely) and so they are probably going to be interested in your advertisement.

You can also target people by general interest, as well. So, in addition to targeting people that have liked Whole Foods, we could search for people that have liked organic foods and possibly people that have liked pages related to health.

You want to make your audience as specific as possible. When you make a more narrow focus, then you are more likely to get a large number of click-throughs.

As you narrow your audience down by page likes and interests, you are going to see your demographics change. Pay close attention to this and note it down. Be sure to save your audience. When you actually create your advertisements, you are going to be able to use the audience by clicking on Saved Audience.

Ad Type and Goal

When you create an advertisement, there are many different advertisement goals you can pursue. We will discuss two of them that are relevant to the kinds of businesses that we are discussing in this book. The first type of advertisement you can run is a page likes campaign. When you do this, you are going to associate your Facebook page with the ad. The purpose of the ad is specifically to drive Facebook users to your page. When they like it, this is similar to "friending" someone on Facebook. From then on, unless they unlike the page, every time you put up a post, it's going to show up on their own Facebook feed. Their friends and family will see it if they go to that person's Facebook feed, so this is a great way to expand your audience.

In the beginning, when you have just started a Facebook page, a likes campaign for a few days is a good idea. That way, you can get the page off the ground by getting an audience built.

The second type of ad that you are going to want to run on Facebook is a traffic campaign. The goal of a traffic campaign is to drive external traffic from Facebook to your website. If you have a storefront like a Shopify store, you can send them directly there. If you have an email landing page, then you can use that as the destination link.

Do not try to use affiliate marketing links in Facebook ads. They don't permit it, and doing so can actually get your ad account suspended or terminated. If you are selling affiliate products, we recommend that you create an email landing page that offers a free video or report if people sign up for your "newsletter," and then you can promote the affiliate offer from your emails after they have signed up. The landing page shouldn't give any indication that you are selling affiliate products, but it should definitely convey the niche that the affiliate product is involved in. Facebook allows ads that target email signup landing pages.

Budget

Facebook will suggest a budget of something on the order of $40 a day. But don't start off with that amount. In fact, you might not ever need it. One of the great things about Facebook advertising is that you can reach a significant level of customers on small budgets. So, start off with a budget of between $2-$5 per day. That sounds crazy, but it usually works.

After the ad has started running, you can gradually increase the budget until you get a level of traffic that you want to sustain. Remember that Facebook has 2.5 billion users, so the chances of you running out of customers in short order is next to nothing. You aren't going to reach more than a hundred or a couple hundred people per day if you are spending $5, but that is going to be enough to start driving significant numbers of email signups and possibly a couple of sales a day if your sales funnel is in good shape. If you find that it's working, then slowly increase the budget. Don't increase it more than fifty cents per day. You can also set up some variations of the ad so that you can do A/B testing. This can include different Facebook ads and also different landing pages. Then after 3-5 days, you simply kill what isn't working and then start increasing the budgets for those advertisements that do work.

When you are testing, you are going to want to look for failure at different points in the lifecycle. So, are you getting a lot of people clicking through, but they aren't signing up for the email? Maybe the copy or images on your landing page are not very good. Alternatively, are they not clicking through to the website? Then maybe the text or media used in your ad are not very good. Take a look at these things and make adjustments as necessary.

Media

Facebook allows you to create a few different types of ads. The default type of ad is a single image, and believe it or not; this still works very well. You can also run video ads, which work very well also. There is also the possibility of making an on the fly video ad from still images using their technology, which will add text and some interesting effects to the manufactured video. We haven't tried this one yet, but it looks like it could be very effective. They also have slide show ads, which can show multiple images or a carousel that can mix images and videos.

In our view, simple is best. We are really not impressed with the idea of making someone go through multiple videos and images unless you are trying to push multiple products in one ad, like showing them that you sell many different t-shirts on your website. Single image ads work very well for driving traffic if the image is relevant and done well. Video ads, of course, do work extremely well.

You can use your own images, but Facebook also makes stock images from Shutterstock available for use without charge.

Platform Options

You can advertise on Facebook feeds, in messaging, in stories, on the right-hand side, and on Instagram. The default option is to advertise everywhere, and we recommend that *you* start with this and then kill any options that are not producing. For some of the ads that we have run, for example, we got many clicks for ads that were shown in the Facebook feed, but very few on Instagram and so we cut Instagram. Facebook provides very comprehensive reporting, and so you will be able to get a clear picture of what is working and what isn't working.

YouTube Advertising

YouTube advertising is another low-cost way to reach a large number of people. With YouTube advertising, you don't even have to create anything special for an ad if you don't want to, provided that you have videos on your channel ready to use.

YouTube advertising, surprisingly enough, is about video. So, you are going to make a video that you want to use in an advertisement and then upload it to your channel, or if you have a video already up there that you think is suitable, then you can use that instead. For videos that you want to advertise with, shorter is better. A 30 second to one-minute video is ideal for making an advertisement.

An advertisement can be sophisticated or not. People on YouTube are not going to be put off by a regular video that they are used to seeing on the site anyway. The point is to put up a good video that people are going to find compelling enough to watch.

In your video, one thing that you want to do is include a call to action. So, this is either going to be you telling them to click to go to your website or putting up a screen in the video with text that tells them where to go.

Leveraging Videos

The fun starts after you have uploaded the video that you are planning to use in your ad. You are going to be taken to a web page where you can specify the usual information, such as daily budget, keywords to target, and so forth. One of the most interesting features of the advertising interface is that you can pick specific videos where your ad is going to run. So, you can pick videos that have large numbers of views, so that you can be assured of having a large audience for your advertisement. When doing this, be sure to do some research ahead of time. You want to find out when videos were uploaded and whether or not they are getting current views or if they racked up a lot of views in the past. If a video has 2 million views, but it got that five years ago, then it is not going to be useful for this purpose. A video that has only been up a week and has 100,000 views is probably going to be more useful.

You can select multiple videos to use. You don't want to use too many but select between 3-10 videos.

Budget

A good thing about advertising on YouTube is that it's a low budget activity. So, you can reach a lot of people for pennies on the dollar. In our testing, we have set budgets of $5 a day and gotten thousands of views. We don't know how it's going to work out in your case, but you should be able to advertise on YouTube without having to spend huge amounts of money.

Chapter 9:

Passive Income

If you are reading this book, then you are definitely convinced of the value of using social media to get followers. However, what is the end goal? The end goal for many is to set up a largely passive income stream. Of course, nothing is going to be entirely passive, but you can get a passive income stream in the sense that you are only going to have to work an hour or two a day at the most once you get everything set up and running.

Work Now, Payoff Later

The most important part of a passive income stream is to put in work now that is going to pay off in the future. If you are putting quality content, whether it is on your blog, your YouTube channel, Instagram, or your Facebook page, it is going to be out there on the internet, getting traffic for months and years to come. As long as all of your links are working, and your users are being directed to working landing pages and sales pages, this means that months and years after you have set these pages up and put posts on social media, they are going to be generating sales and income for you.

As time goes on, if you are continually adding content, and therefore getting viewed by search engines like Google as an authority, you are going to be driving more and more organic traffic. You will probably always want to include advertising as a part of your approach, but you are going to find that as time goes on, you are getting higher levels of organic income.

One of the mistakes that a lot of people make is that they think they are going to get organic traffic right away, but then it doesn't happen, and so they think the business is a failure. This is a huge mistake because organic traffic is something that builds up slowly – but surely – over an extended time period providing that you keep adding to your content. The key to success is quality content that has a lot of value.

In most cases, organic traffic works in exponential fashion. An exponential curve starts off with a very slow rise, and then it suddenly accelerates to high values. This is how organic web traffic often works. In the first weeks and months of your efforts, it's going to seem like you are getting nowhere because you are only going to have a trickle of traffic. But if you are persistent and stick with it, months down the road, you are going to start seeing your traffic increase rapidly.

Consistency Is the Key

Setting up both a daily and weekly routine to post for your business is going to be an important part of getting a passive income to work. Continually posting content is a large part of the secret to success. So, you want to have a routine where you always follow the same steps so that nothing gets neglected. The specific ways that you post are not as important as setting up a posting routine and then carrying it out. Here is a sample routine:

- Post to Facebook : 3 times a week, on Tuesday, Thursday, and Saturday.

- Post to Twitter: At least once per day.

- Post to Instagram: Twice per day.

- Post to Pinterest: Monday and Friday.

- Post to blog: Sunday, Tuesday, and Thursday. Post blog posts on Facebook and Twitter.

- Post video to YouTube: Once a week, every Thursday.

The specifics in this plan can work for some people, but they really don't matter, come up with your own schedule if you like. Some may not use Pinterest, and in its place, you can post another video to YouTube. The value of regular posting, however, can't be said enough. This has two benefits. The first is getting you into a disciplined habit of continually adding content. This is the most important factor for growing passive income that is going to come from organic traffic. The second factor is adding some anticipation for your followers on social media.

Using YouTube as an example, as you get better at making videos and get channel subscribers, people are going to start anticipating your videos if they are passionate about your niche. As you build a following, and you start dropping videos every Monday and Thursday, say, your following is going to eagerly anticipate the arrival of your videos. That is going to help drive views. If you are using advertising to monetize your channel, that is going to help you earn more money, and you will also be getting regular visits to your main website and other social media sites.

If your content is compelling, then your subscribers are going to be sharing it with their friends, helping you to grow even more and get extra free traffic.

Free and Paid Traffic Leads to Passive Income

For passive income, that doesn't mean you never work at all. It means that you are not working a 40-hour workweek or even 20 hours. It doesn't take long to set up a Facebook ad, and after that, all you have to do is occasionally check it to keep tabs on things and make occasional adjustments. In the meantime, every day, the ads are going to be driving hundreds of people to your websites, and some people are going to be buying your products. After the ad is established, then you are only going to have to spend 10 or 20 minutes checking out results, and it might be generating $100-$300 a day in income for you.

Finding Offers to Sell

Running a passive income business is something that is more suitable for electronic products. These are products that are sold and consumed online, so they are information products. They can be how-to guides, training courses, or software. Once they are made, you don't have to worry about maintaining them. It is also possible to set up a drop shipping business, but that is a bit more work.

Let's talk about information products first, and about the idea of creating your own information products. Keep in mind that you don't have to create your own information products. As we will see in a minute, there are plenty of places to find products that you can sell as an affiliate, and you can actually make really good money doing so. But there are some drawbacks to being an affiliate, which is something that we are also going to discuss.

The first thing to think about is whether or not you know enough about a subject to make an information product. In most cases, the answer is yes. The reason is that you only have to know a little bit more than the general public knows. You can start with things that you are passionate about now. Is there any way that you could turn that passion into teaching about it? Again, you don't have to be a doctor to do it.

There are two ways that you can go about it. The first and easiest way is to create a book in PDF format. Then you can sell the book online. Depending on how extensive the book is, you can charge anywhere from $17-$27. Many people are going to say, "what about Kindle"? That is a valid question, but the truth is if you write a book and then publish it on major bookstores, you are going to make pennies. To make a living that way, you have to publish a large number of books. They only sell for $2.99, and most books are free to read, but you get paid by the online store, fractions of a penny per page. This isn't to say that the model can't work, but unless you want to write and publish a huge number of books, that is not going to be something that many people are going to be interested in pursuing. With the online model, you can be making up to $47 per sale.

The second option is more lucrative and provides more value to the customer, and therefore you can charge more money. This method is to create a video course. Depending on the subject and how much value your course provides, you can charge anywhere from $47 all the way up to $1,000 or more. You can host your course on a website called Kajabi, that offers a full-blown suite of tools for businesses that are selling video education courses. They manage everything for you, including having a comment system, ways to drip release your video course, quizzes, and a setup for people to contact you for support. They also have a login system that will assign your users' login names and passwords, and they manage the security. This isn't an advertisement for Kajabi, and we are just letting readers know that there are full-blown sites available so that you don't have to reinvent the wheel, as far as having a secured video course website.

Affiliate Marketing

Now let's talk about affiliate marketing. For many readers, the idea of creating your own video course sounds intimidating, and it might not even be something that you want to do. The good news is that there are many affiliate marketing courses that can be used to sell physical and digital goods online. JVZoo and ClickBank are two that are worth checking out. You can find affiliate products in nearly every niche on these sites, and many that pay out high commissions.

When you visit ClickBank, as an example, you can go to their marketplace. You can either browse by category or search by specific keywords. On ClickBank, they also provide a useful metric called gravity. This tells you how many affiliates sold at least one copy of a product over the past 12 weeks. The rule of thumb is that any product that has a gravity of 20 and above is worth promoting. There are some very strong products that have gravity scores over 200, but one of the downsides of high gravity products is that this also means that a ton of people are on the internet promoting the product. If you are late to the game, the buying public might be saturated, having seen the product offered to them by a bunch of people many times. A high gravity product has also probably been advertised on Facebook many times.

There are other ways to sell affiliate products, as well. Many services like Bluehost web hosting will pay you an affiliate commission if you get someone to sign up for their service. You can also sell Amazon products as an affiliate, but the commissions in these cases are going to be a lot lower than what you get selling something like a ClickBank product, where you can earn $20 up to hundreds of dollars per sale.

So, let's talk about the advantages of affiliate products. The first advantage is a big one – it saves you the hassle of creating your own product from scratch. The second advantage is you can find products that are already market-tested. Typically, a ClickBank product owner has put a large amount of effort into building out their website and researching the niche so that they know it is something that can get large numbers of sales. Another advantage is often ClickBank sellers will provide you with many selling tools that you can use. So, you can use their emails that are proven to convert, and they may have many product images, banners, logos, and other materials that you can use to promote the product.

There are some downsides to ClickBank products as well. One of them is that affiliate marketing links are frowned upon by many websites. This includes Facebook, unfortunately, and if you try to run an ad on Facebook that goes directly to an affiliate marketing link, you are likely to have the ad pulled (if it is approved at all) and you might even get your account suspended or terminated, depending on what kind of affiliate offer you were promoting. One thing to watch out for is internet marketing training courses. In other words, there are a lot of people out there who sell courses that teach people how to set up and run an Internet business. To get an idea of what we are talking about, go on Google and look up "John Cristani." Now is John Cristani legitimate? We believe he is completely legitimate. The problem is not him, but Facebook simply doesn't allow you to advertise for the type of training that he provides. They have labeled it a "get rich quick" scheme, and they are very strict about it.

That means that if you are selling an affiliate product, you are going to have to put some work in to create your own website. Hopefully, you have one already, but all you need for the purposes of selling an affiliate product is a landing page.

Another downside to selling affiliate products is that you are going to be competing with a significant number of other people selling the same product. That means that you are going to have a harder time breaking through to get sales of your own. When you are posting videos about it on YouTube, there might be ten or twenty other people doing the same thing.

One thing that can work in your favor, however, is most affiliate marketers are not very good (although there are definitely some real pros out there). This is something that you can observe on YouTube on a regular basis. When a new product is released, you will see the amateurs simply post a video on YouTube that they stole or borrowed (or even used with permission) from the owner of the product, and they don't offer any real value of their own. One thing that we can advise is that if you are selling affiliate marketing products, you can give yourself a real edge if you offer some value of your own.

This can be done in many different ways. For starters, instead of just slapping yet another copy of the same video on YouTube, make your own video that offers some value that is directly related to the niche. If you are serious about marketing the product, get the product and offer a real, genuine review of it. In many cases, the seller on ClickBank will give you a review copy, but those are harder to get than they used to be because many affiliates abused the privilege and posted them for download online. But if you are attempting to make a serious effort at starting a business that is built around the product, then buying it so that you can genuinely review it is probably a worthwhile investment.

There are several ways you can publish reviews. Publish one on your blog, provided that you have a blog that is directly related to the niche. You can also post your reviews on social media sites. This step would suppose that you have a good, usually non-salesy relationship with your followers. This is where the trust that you build up over time with your social media followers can come into play. If you are a trusted voice in the niche, and you are providing good content to your social media followers that has a lot of actionable value on a regular basis, it will be OK to periodically recommend an affiliate product. And since they trust you, many of your followers are probably going to end up buying the product. But don't abuse your position. If you push a bad product, that will destroy the trust that you have spent so much time building up with your users. If you put up a lot of spammy posts that simply try to sell an affiliate product, that is going to turn off a lot of your followers, and many of them will drop out and unfollow you, unfriend you, and unsubscribe. So, when it comes to pushing affiliate marketing products on social media sites, remember that less is often more.

Another way to promote affiliate marketing products that works quite well is to put up a website that reviews related products. Then post a long, thorough, and genuine review of the product. You can incorporate a video from YouTube in the review, but be sure to target the right keywords and include a lot of text. These days, Google is also giving points for having a few images on your web page, as well. They recognize that people are attracted by visual content, so sometimes a web page that has a couple of images placed among the text is going to do better than one that is just text alone.

So how much can you make as an affiliate marketer? The cold hard truth is most people make little to no money. But the reason that they don't make any money is that they fail to put the effort required, or they make bad decisions like posting the same exact video 30 others posted. If you take it seriously and learn the skills necessary to build a business with it, you can make anywhere from $50,000 up to $1 million a year.

Chapter 10:

Sales Methods

In this chapter, we are going to talk about closing a sale, with techniques that are going to be useful whether or not you have your own product or are pushing an affiliate marketing product. Something that is interesting is these techniques were developed many years ago, but they still work very well.

When the Internet first got started, it was possible to run a pay per click ad on Google or Yahoo and include an affiliate link directly in the ad, and so you could get easy sales just pushing traffic to a sales page for a product. For some reason, the powers that be in Google decided that this was unacceptable behavior. So, they began to ban direct linking via affiliate links. We have seen similar behavior by others, such as Facebook.

Marketers needed to come up with a new strategy, and by 2008 people were using email marketing to great effect. This was used before that, of course, but it was around that time that it became the standard go-to marketing method. Today, it is as widespread as ever, and almost every website that you visit is going to have some kind of email signup form.

Email Marketing

So, what is email marketing? Email marketing uses emails combined with affiliate links (or links to your own product pages) that push traffic in the hopes of making sales. It has a high conversion rate, because people have to voluntarily sign up to join your email list. If you are honest about what the purpose of the email list is, then you are likely to be able to drive sales from it. So, what do we mean when we say being honest? That means that you are using your email list for the same niche that you told people about in the first place. Each email list that you create should be for one specific niche and not discuss unrelated topics.

An email marketing scheme will send people multiple emails after they sign up for your newsletter or whatever you want to call it. Typically, you will send out emails every day for a few days, and then start tapering off the frequency. If you want to build up a large list and keep it going for a long time, you might want to periodically email them about important news or tips related to the niche topic.

In your emails, you don't always want to do a hard sell. The first email should be a long email that has a lot of discussion about the niche topic. Then at the end of the email, you can recommend the product you are selling with a link. You should continue this approach for a couple of emails after that, and then you can send out an email with a hard sell. The truth is, after this point, if people have not purchased, most of them are not going to, but sometimes you do get some late adopters.

To have an email marketing system, you are not going to manually send out the emails, that would be far too much work. The way you want to do it is using an autoresponder service. They will collect the email addresses for you from customers and send out your emails at regular intervals each time a customer signs up. Some of the good autoresponder services that are available include Get Response, AWeber, and Mail Chimp.

Sales Funnel

An email marketing campaign is something that is a part of what is called a sales funnel. A sales funnel is just a small number of websites that are used to close a sale. The first page that people are going to encounter in the funnel is a signup form where you offer them a free gift in exchange for signing up for your email list. The free gift can be a short book or a video mini-course. The point is to offer them some real value in order to get them to sign up for your email list.

When they sign up, they will be directed to the second web page that is in the funnel. There are different ways you can set this up, and some people actually send the customer directly to the sales page of the product after they sign up for the newsletter. Alternatively, you can have them go to a second page that does a little "preselling" of the product. For example, you could have your review of an affiliate product posted here. The page will have buttons or links on it to take them to the sales page if they are interested.

If they are not interested, it's not a big deal because now you have their email address, and you can email them at any time. So, you can email them and use more gentle persuasion to buy the product or to sell other products to them. The same general principle applies, don't be too salesy in your approach. If people are getting a lot of hard sell emails in their inbox, then they will either stop reading your emails or, worse, unsubscribe from the list altogether.

The sales funnel can also be used to push more offers, called upsells. So, you can have additional steps in the funnel. You can try and sell people more expensive products in the same niche using the other pages in the funnel, or "downsell" them by offering them a book or something that is cheaper. These methods have been tested over and over again, and if you set it up right, they work. Of course, doing it right means having a nice-looking website and the right sales copy. If you are not sure about this or don't have much experience, try looking at what other people are doing to get some examples of how to set things up.

There are many services that you can use to set up a sales funnel using drag and drop functionality. There is no reason to try and build a website from scratch when everything is already made for you. One service to strongly consider is called Get Response. The reason that a lot of marketers like Get Response is that it incorporates the ability to build a sales funnel with an email autoresponder.

One of the best services for building a sales funnel is called ClickFunnels. This site was designed by expert internet marketers who made their first million on ClickBank as affiliates. So, they know exactly what is needed to build a sales funnel, and they provide it for you. It comes with a large number of drag and drop templates that make it easy, and you can incorporate the pages you create into a blog or website, or you can have them hosted there and even register new domain names. You can set up email autoresponders in the service, but it is better, in our opinion, to use an external email autoresponder like AWeber or Mail Chimp, and this can be integrated into your ClickFunnels projects quite easily.

Driving Traffic

Of course, a sales funnel isn't any good without traffic. We have actually talked a great deal about driving traffic already, that is what your social media presence is ultimately for. You can have your sales funnel as the link on your Instagram profile, you can link to it every time that you post a YouTube video, and you can link to it from your blog and from Facebook.

Paid traffic can also be used in conjunction with a sales funnel. Of course, you can use Facebook ad campaigns to drive traffic to a sales funnel. You can also use old-time pay-per-click advertising. Google and Yahoo/Bing can both be used. Bing doesn't appeal as much to people, but Bing will drive a large amount of traffic to our sites. The traffic on Bing is generally quite a bit cheaper than you have to spend to advertise on Google.

There are also some other options that can be used for paid advertising, but many of them are of dubious value. One possibility that is frequently discussed is "network" advertising. These are ads that you see on many websites that are often square-shaped with an image and some text below. They are found on many major websites, but the problem with this type of advertising is that it is not well-targeted. As a hypothetical example, suppose that you are running these types of ads, but they are being displayed on generic websites like CNN, say. In that case, the overall audience is very large, but the downside is that very few people in that audience are going to be interested in your niche. Generally, a niche is going to apply to a small subset of the overall population, but most people are not going to be very interested. So, your ad is going to be showing for no real purpose. If you are paying for impressions, then you are going to go bankrupt very fast because you could get a lot of impressions on those big websites without getting any clicks or sales.

What you want is targeted advertising. Search engine advertising works because people are searching for related keywords that you specify when you create the ad. So those people are already interested in the topic to begin with, and many of those people are actually on the search engines because they are interested in buying a product that is going to help them solve a problem that is related to that niche.

On Facebook or Instagram, you can target people who have demonstrated in the past that they are interested in a particular niche, by liking Facebook pages that are related to your niche in some way. So, if you are going to use paid traffic, our suggestion is to use Google PPC, YouTube, Bing, and Facebook. Between these networks (which also covers Instagram), you have covered literally everyone in the general public.

You can also, when appropriate, directly advertise on other social media sites like Pinterest. Before you do so, be sure that people that are using the site that you pick are interested in your product or service in some way. Remember that on Pinterest, the audience is largely female, and so if you are selling something that men only are interested in, then you are not going to have very much success with your advertising efforts on that site.

There are other tricks that you can try to use for promotion. One that has been suggested by some internet marketers is a social media contest. You can run a Facebook contest, or an Instagram giveaway to try and generate some hype among your followers. When you are doing this, hopefully, your current followers will share the information and bring in some new prospects that will become followers and possibly visit your sales funnel and sign up for the email list.

There are some older tricks that people have also used to varying degrees of success. One method that has worked for *some* people is posting craigslist ads for affiliate marketing products they are selling. This may or may not work depending on luck. The good thing about this approach is that it is free, and Craigslist gets a huge amount of traffic. The bad thing about this is the site is policed by independent zealots that will flag your post as inappropriate. If that happens, the ad will be taken down, but you could even get "banned" from the site, although you might be able to sneak back on using a different email address.

We haven't tried this method, but we have known people that got a lot of sales doing it. A different approach may be to try it without using a direct affiliate link. That might not offend the hardcore people that are on Craigslist as much as an affiliate link would. But again, keep in mind that we haven't tried it, so try at your own risk!

Summary

An email list is a central part of closing the sale, once you have driven traffic to your website. The gateway to your website is going to be a sales funnel. The sales funnel takes the customer through several steps to encourage them to purchase products. Social media and paid advertising are the best ways to get traffic to your sales funnel so that you can get customers to sign up and buy your products and services. You can also try other "guerilla marketing" methods.

Conclusion

Thank you for making it through to the end of Influencer Marketing, let's hope it was informative and able to provide you with all of the tools you need to achieve your goals whatever they may be.

If you have made it all the way through the book, you will have a more thorough understanding of social media, what sites are the most important, and how to utilize them in order to drive traffic to your business and build a solid following.

Reading a book is only the first step. Now that you have some idea of what to do, you should get started building your business. One of the unfortunate things about our era is that despite the wealth of information that is available, and all of the tools that can be exploited to reach customers, is the fact that only a small fraction of people that take courses, read books, or follow videos on starting a new business online ever take action. Simply taking action is an important step on the road to success. If you don't try, of course, you are not going to fail, and you can keep doing what you are doing now. But among those who take the appropriate steps, many are going to reach a new level of success.

We sincerely hope that we have provided our readers with a significant amount of actionable information. It isn't necessary to get on every social media website or app, and in fact, it's better to establish a solid presence on a few key sites.

In our view, the next steps are to start by preparing yourself properly to deal with a flow of customers first. That means setting up your sales funnel, having a clear sales message and lead magnet, and then having a systematic way to connect your social media posting and advertising to the sales funnel.

Once you have that step-down, you can use paid advertising to start driving traffic immediately. Once you launch paid advertising on social media, you are going to find that it is nearly instant. You can use this to your advantage if things are not working out right away, and if you find that you don't get instant success, don't get discouraged. If things are not working out, take a close look at your sales funnel, and make adjustments. You might have to make changes to the colors or images used on your site, or perhaps change your sales copy. Test, test, and test again is one bit of advice that you should remember when it comes to marketing.

If you are looking to improve your education, there are many resources that are available online. You can find many of these resources free of charge. On YouTube, there are many expert marketers who make free videos that can help you learn how to make an income online. You can also find people that will teach you how to use social media websites and apps in order to build your own following, and then how to leverage it to drive traffic to your own sales funnel, where you can turn eyeballs into paying customers.

Finally, you can also utilize the educational site Udemy, where many experts offer their advice in reasonably priced courses. But most of all, besides educating yourself, be sure to take action! Best of luck to all of our readers!

Finally, if you found this book useful in any way, a review on Amazon is always appreciated!

SOCIAL MEDIA
MARKETING TRICKS
2020

INTRODUCTIONS

Facebook, Twitter, Instagram and YouTube; names that come to mind when we talk about social networks (RRSS). Those are the 4 best known, but today there are so many that it is impossible to find a complete list.

They are part of our day to day, and an increasingly important part, so it is convenient to know them. To know what a social network is we can go to a dictionary.

Social network is defined as a service of the information society that offers users a communication platform through the Internet so that they generate a profile with their personal data, facilitating the creation of communities based on criteria common and allowing the communication of its users so that they can interact through messages, share information, images or videos, allowing these publications to be immediately accessible by all users in your group.

A very complete definition but a little dense, so we go with a more affordable definition and of walking around the house:

A social network is a digital space in which users interact, communicating with each other or sharing information.

Thanks to social networks, users form communities based on common interests, friendship relationships or professional relationships. Depending on the user's objectives (which can be a real person or a brand), social networks can be categorized into:

Generic social networks, which aim to socialize through the Internet, Professional social networks, which work to connect colleagues or to look for work.

Thematic social networks, which are reduced to a specific topic (there are social networks for lovers of cinema, photography, fashion).

CHAPTER
ONE

SOCIAL MEDIA OR SOCIAL NETWORKS

You probably already got confused between networks and social media. But it is important to clarify that they are not the same thing. Therefore, we are going to differentiate them right now.

As I told you, social networks are the groups of connections and relationships we have with other people. And social media are platforms that guarantee that happens.

Still confused? It is clear when we understand that both can serve as platforms to maintain our networks of relationships, however, social networks have that as their main feature and are within what we classify as social media.

While social media are platforms that have as their main function, the mass exchange of content and transmission of information, such as blogs, pages and even YouTube itself.

Summing up all that, we can affirm that social networks are a category within social media. Places where we can interact with people we know, but in which at all times we are exposed to an immensity of content.

SOCIAL MEDIA TRACKING

Your work does not end when you press the submit button. The truth is this is just the beginning. You need to be aware of everything that happens in your social networks and that is why I will talk about what you need to be aware of and good practices:

Comments

They are very important for your strategy and show who is willing to interact with your brand. Therefore, if someone cared enough to comment something, like or react to that comment and respond when necessary. The famous use of gifs is approved, but always with moderation and consistency.

A mention can be very good, as well as sharing a content or praise, but it can also be a bad thing, like someone expressing dissatisfaction with your company. Stay tuned for this! In the end, this person shared the content and that can be propagated. Respond with sincerity and solve the situation.

Evaluations

You probably saw the evaluation of a page on Facebook. And despite being present only in this network, evaluations deserve your attention. In the end, they serve as a thermometer of how people are considering your brand and are public.

Occasionally something negative may arise, but one of the main virtues of any social media professional is to remain calm and resolve that situation efficiently.

It shows sensitivity and guarantees that this problem will be solved. People want to feel empowered and heard. Remember it!

Chat

Currently the chats in social networks, whatever they are, function as the SAC 2.0 model in social networks. And that is where most of the time a consumer will solve their doubts, seek help, solve some question or express some dissatisfaction.

This is perhaps one of the most important spaces of social networks, it is a personal contact you have with a certain user, and the impression you leave represents the image of your brand for him.

SOCIAL NETWORK METRICS

If you came here without understanding the importance of data and analysis of results for a social media strategy, I failed my mission. But I will solve this by showing you now what metrics you need to accompany to ensure your success. Join me a little more:

Scope

The scope is what will show how many users your post reached. This does not mean that they interacted with the publication or stopped reading it.

So why is this important to you? Because it will help you understand how your posts are performing according to the Facebook algorithm.

Based on this analysis you will be able to adapt your strategy and optimize what is necessary for your publications to reach your audience.

Traffic

If your social networks are not bringing traffic to your website or blog in any way, you are doing something very wrong. Understanding how you take a user through the funnel of your company is essential and social networks have a very important role: the acquisition.

Interest

It is here that you see who are the true followers of your brand and who is willing to interact with you. But what does interest really mean? It is the number of likes, shares and comments that your posts have.

It is going to show you mainly how relevant and attractive your strategy has been, in addition to helping you interact with your audience.

Channel growth

The larger your fan base, the more people you have the chance to reach. But, this can be a treacherous number, because not always the growth of your channel will mean a growth of interest or scope. It is important you put more effort as that is what will make it possible.

Vanity Metrics

When talking about treacherous, we need to talk about vanity metrics. Do you know what they are? Basically, they are numbers that will surely leave you happy, you should not feel guilty about it but they do not bring real results for your company.

Did your post have 5000 likes? Congratulations, you probably deserved it. But that will not help you make any decisions and does not provide insights about future actions. Then you can accompany them, just don't spend so much time with them.

If you got here Congratulations! We hope you can take advantage of everything learned to take your social media strategy to another level and multiply your results.

But as we well know, it is never enough and surely you can still discover more about this incredible world of social networks. To always take this knowledge wherever you go and consult it when you need, I recommend you download our checklist so you don't miss anything on your social media profile.

STRATEGIES FOR SOCIAL MEDIA MARKETING

There are many possibilities in social media marketing. The individual social networks offer different forms to be present in the network. But behind all these uses is a common social media strategy. Before you go You should ask yourself the following questions about your company and social network products:

- Situation analysis?
- What does the target group look like?
- What are the goals you want to achieve?
- Which channel is suitable for this?
- Which resources are there?
- How can I perform a success check?

Situation analysis

The first is the question of which social network you are already using. Are these enough or do I need to revise them? How does your competition work on social media? If the use of social media marketing is already common in the industry, you need to work harder to implement the strategy. You also need to know the time and money you can spend pursuing social media strategies.

Target group

The important point is the target audience. If you know who is most likely to use your product or service, you need to know where this viewer is on the social media platform. If you know who you want to deal with, you can get clear images of individual content forms.

Goal definition

Clearly defined goals facilitate the implementation of each strategy. Your main goal may be to sell your product, but it should not be the focus of a social media strategy. This overflows with each user's time. However, one goal is to build a brand, acquire new customers, build efficient customer service, or communicate with customers as fans.

Channel selection

When choosing the right social media channel, you must head towards the target group. For example, if your audience is primarily focused on video content and images, you will need to adjust the content accordingly. You can also create videos about the product and provide informational videos. For example, the YouTube platform is perfect for this.

Resource

This includes both time and financial budgets. After all, working on social media requires almost daily employment. You need to post regularly or respond to user requests. You'll also need to clarify in advance how much you'll invest in banner ads and content boost. A professional social media manager should help as soon as you need two or three social media networks.

Success control

Each marketing metric also requires a review of success. ROI is used for social media marketing, which is also part of online marketing. This return on investment shows the amount of profit generated by social media marketing measures is compared to their cost.

Examples of social media strategies

Social media campaigns are most successful when they spread automatically. Postings that go viral are the best solution for social media marketing. Whether content becomes viral or not can not be predicted. There is no panacea, but there are some strategies that offer the highest chances to make a campaign viral.

The online marketing mix

Online Marketing pursues the goals of increasing the visibility of its own company and increasing the number of visitors on the Internet. This happens with the right marketing mix. The following components are available for this:

Website or Conversion Rate Optimization (CRO)

SEM and SEO (Search Engine Marketing or Optimization)

Content Marketing

Social Media Marketing

E-mail marketing

Affiliate Marketing

Viral Campaign Marketing

Online PR

Website - or conversion rate optimization (CRO)

The website tracks multiple destinations simultaneously. It is primarily there to generate sales but also to increase the commitment of users. This means that users can order your products on your website and they can search through your assortment. You can also offer interesting downloads on your website and introduce your company in detail. With Conversion Rate Optimization you can improve your website in terms of the user journey and simplify the actions of the users you want on your site.

SEM

This abbreviation stands for Search Engine Marketing. This method includes SEA (Search Engine Advertisement) and SEO (Search Engine Optimization). Especially keywords play a crucial role. But also internal links within your website, technical aspects as well as link building (generating backlinks) are part of it.

Content Marketing

Content Marketing deals with the content that can be found on your website. This can be texts or pictures, but also videos or livestreams. In any case, this content should offer added value for the user as well as being interesting and up-to-date. Not for nothing is mentioned always and everywhere: Content is King. If your content is not worth reading and offers no added value, users will lose in large quantities.

Social Media Marketing

Social media marketing deals with the dissemination of corporate content on the pages of social networks. So it's also part of online marketing.

E-mail marketing

E-mail marketing sends e-mails or newsletters at regular intervals. While e-mail marketing was the undisputed number one in direct contact with customers a few years ago, the marketing channel is now facing competition from messenger marketing via Facebook

Messenger, What's App and Co., which is also made possible by social media

Affiliate Marketing

This is understood as an online marketing system operated by commercial providers. This provider remunerates its distribution partners with commissions. The provider provides advertising material that the affiliate marketer can use. If this use leads to purchase agreements, the marketer receives a commission.

Viral campaign marketing

Viral marketing primarily uses the social network to spread advertising messages. One of the hallmarks of marketing that becomes viral is the rapid spread on the Internet. An interesting and usually strange message is clicked in a kind of chain reaction and made viral. The term comes from medicine, when viruses as pathogens have a rapid spread.

Online PR

Online PR is a form of modern public relations. Content is not communicated via traditional channels such as TV or radio, but over the Internet. Online PR specializes in a social network such as Twitter.

To look for a suitable social network, it is advisable to look at the statistics. The Hamburg-based communications consultancy Faktenkontor, for example, together with the market research institute Toluna, has recently examined the usage habits of Germans. Advertising on social networks is as good as advertising on TV. Above all, Facebook advertising dominates. About a quarter of all Germans felt led by Facebook advertising to buy a product. Around 20% of YouTube users purchased a product or used a service as a result of advertising. The platform as a social network thus lies in the advertising hyperspace between print media and the radio.

Age-specific, there are also differences in the frequency of use of individual social networks. Snapchat and Instagram are very popular with young people in particular. Around 71% of all users between the ages of 14 and 19 use these networks. But also Pinterest is in high demand among the young people. More than a third use this platform as a social network.

For the older users, ages 30 and up, Xing and LinkedIn are at the top of the list.

How much does Social Media Marketing cost ?

The cost of social media marketing depends primarily on the needs of your business. A lump sum, which must be spent for it, there is just as little as in conventional advertising. However, all social media-related activities require staffing. Websites must be maintained and user requests must be responded to. This requires constant attention to the topic as well as a permanent presence in the social media. This personnel expenditure costs above all time and money.

Certainly, viral marketing is the cheapest. Videos that become viral are self-tracking. But that does not happen without previous planning and good content.

Companies that already have a PR department recruiting their own staff. Others set up their own department. A third option is to hire an external marketing agency.

If you now calculate all the resulting costs, you can expect that a social media campaign will require at least a budget of 10,000 euros. The individual possibilities you see here again briefly summarized.

Recruitment of own staff

Establishment of a separate department

Commissioning of an external agency

IDENTIFYING WINNING STRATEGIES FOR MARKETING ON SOCIAL MEDIA

Here's how to design your social networking strategy in steps:

- Identify your goals
- Identify your target audiences
- Select the right platforms
- Master the algorithms
- Adopt the right content strategy
- Monitor and improve your performance

1. Identify your goals

Social media is a channel of promotion and not an end in itself. The social networking strategy is part of a much broader context: your web marketing strategy. In order to be effective, your strategic social media plan must be aligned with the growth objectives of your SME in the long and short term.

That's why the first step in any social media strategy is to determine what you hope to gain from your efforts.

What are your strategic goals

Do you want to share your business with people who have never heard of it? Or inspire your current customers to do business with you again?

When it comes to web marketing, your prospective customers can be captured at different stages of their buying process:

- Awareness / Exploration

- Interest / Consideration

- Conversion

- Loyalty

So, your strategic goals will largely depend on the stage at which you want to reach your prospects:

HOW TO USE SOCIAL MEDIA TO ACHIEVE THESE GOALS

No matter which stage of the sales process you want to target, you will be able to use your social media strategy to achieve your goals:

Build your brand awareness: Social media advertising allows you to target the individuals most likely to be interested in your business to showcase your brand.

Convince your prospects: the strategic use of hash tags on social media and the optimization of your video referencing on you tube allow you to capture your prospects when they are actively looking for your products and services.

Generate sales: Integrating a Facebook store or Instagram Shopping allows you to convert your subscribers into customers without having to leave the platform.

Build customer loyalty: With social media, you can continue to interact with your customers after their purchase and even target them with remarketing campaigns on Facebook Ads.

In short: once you have defined your goals, you will be able to identify the actions to take to achieve them and maximize your efforts.

What are your performance indicators

An objective will never be attainable if it is not quantifiable or measurable. KPIs examples you can define in your social media strategy to guide its execution:

Performance indicators for your organic efforts:

- Size of your community
- Scope of your publications
- Commitment
- clicks
- Messages / Calls

Performance indicators for your paid advertising:

- Click through rate
- Conversion rate
- Cost per commitment (mentions "I like", comments, reactions, sharing ...)
- Cost per click

- Cost per call

2. Identify your target audiences

Does your company sell to individuals (B2C) or businesses (B2B)? Are your products or services designed for individuals residing in a specific geographic area?

To answer these questions and more, while still keeping your target audience in mind, we strongly suggest you define a persona in your social media strategy.

What is a persona

This is your typical client profile and its demographic, psychological and behavioral characteristics. When drawing the portrait of your persona, you can include:

- His age
- His sex
- His job
- Where he / she lives
- His interests
- His lifestyle
- Her personality

This type of description gives you a much clearer idea of the needs and expectations of your prospective customers. This makes it easier for you to adapt your editorial tone to your community and create more engaging content to reach your goals quickly.

3. Select the right platforms

Now that your persona is identified, you need to determine the best way to reach them. What social media platforms do they use?

You would not use Instagram, a photo sharing platform, to sell to the blind, or Snapchat to sell to the elderly. In short: make sure you target your potential customers where they are.

Here are some general information to help you choose your platform, among the 7 most popular social networks:

WHO USES FACEBOOK?

- Number of users: 2 billion
- Suitable for B2B and B2C
- Demographic characteristics:
- 56% men / 44% women
- 65% of users are over 35
- Popular in urban and rural environments

WHO USES YOUTUBE?

- Number of users: 1.5 billion
- Suitable for B2B and B2C
- Demographic characteristics:
- 62% of users are men
- 61% are between 16-34 years old

WHO USES INSTAGRAM?

- Number of users: 800 million

- More suitable for B2C

- Demographic characteristics:

- Most popular with women: 38% of women use Instagram, compared to 26% of men.

- Popular among 15-30 years old

- Much more popular with users living in urban areas

WHO USES TWITTER?

- Number of users: 350 million

- Suitable for B2C and B2B

- Demographic characteristics:

- 50-50 Men / Women

- Strong press and influencers / bloggers

- WHO USES SNAPCHAT?

- Number of users: 180 million

- Much better suited to B2C

- Demographic characteristics:

- 70% of users are women

- 70% of users are under 34

WHO USES LINKEDIN?

- Number of users: 106 million
- Much more suitable for B2B
- Demographic characteristics:
- 31% of men and 27% of women use Linkedin
- Strong use of people with high incomes

WHO USES PINTEREST?

- Number of users: 100 million
- Suitable for B2C and B2B
- Demographic characteristics:
- 70% of users are women

You can also use this grid to quickly determine which platforms you should focus on in your social media strategy based on your business profile:

4. Master the algorithms

Once your platforms have been identified and your social networking pages created and optimized

Before you start production, optimization and dissemination of your content, you must first master your platforms ... and more precisely: their algorithms.

These are mathematical formulas used each time a publication is created to determine whether it deserves to be featured on the users' news feed.

As you will have understood, mastering how these algorithms work is a decisive factor in your ability to have good results. Although the algorithms are not all the same, their logic is very similar.

Here are, for example, the criteria on which Edge Rank, the facebook algorithm, is based to disseminate your organic publications:

Affinity: the propensity of users to engage with the content of your page in the past

Performance: the number of likes, reactions, comments, sharing of the publication

The type of content: text, image, video

5. Adopt the right content strategy

Once the algorithm is well understood, you are ready to feed your pages strategically. To do this, you will have to work on three levels: the creation of quality content, the strategic and effective dissemination of this content, and finally the optimization of the conversations it generates.

Here's how to optimize your social media at each of these steps:

- Create quality content
- Talk about what interests your persona
- Generate conversations
- Bet on a superior graphic quality

- Adapt your content to each platform
- Use engaging formats
- Put yourself in ephemeral content
- Enjoy user-generated content
- Adopt good dissemination practices
- Plan your publications
- Publish at the right time
- Use advertising
- Optimize your publications for conversion
- Use influencers
- Encourage making contact

5 Create quality content

Talk about what interests your persona

Nobody wants to go to a dinner party with friends and sit next to someone who only talks about himself ... It's the same on social media.

While the goal of a social media strategy is obviously to use your social networks to promote your business and talk about your products, put yourself in your persona's shoes instead.

What would you like to see on the Company pages that you follow? What type of content would you react to? What kind of publications would you share with your friends? What would challenge you?

To answer all these questions, there is nothing better than including a social media watch in your social networking strategy.

You can also vary your content by applying these tips:

- Promote entertaining, useful or inspiring publications
- Tell stories
- Reveal your imperfections and humanize your business
- Do not be too commercial
- Get out of your comfort zone and introduce new topics from time to time, or try new formats of publications.

B. Generate conversations

Humanize your brand on social media by generating conversations with - and between - your customers.

To do this, offer useful, entertaining or inspiring content that your subscribers will be able to share and want to share. You can also ask questions or ask your subscribers' opinions to stimulate debate or encourage them to share their opinions.

Be sure to respond to comments that your fans take the trouble to leave you: the prospect of getting an answer encourages them to comment again and encourages other subscribers to do the same.

C. Bet on superior graphic quality

The graphic quality of your social media reflects your professionalism and credibility ... Do not take it lightly!

From strategic thinking to execution, you will need to focus on the quality of your publications at every stage of your social media strategy. To ensure you provide satisfying content, here are some good practices to follow:

Make sure to re-read your texts: are they persona oriented? Are they useful for your fans? Do they contain errors? Check the quality of the visual or video content: does it represent your brand? Is it rich and well done? Is it adapted to the social media platform used?

Follow the best practices of each platform: emojis, hashtags, targeting, hours of publication etc. In order to be well armed for the production of quality content on your social networks, we recommend the following tools:

By applying these tips and using the right tools, we are confident that you will stand out from your competition and get the attention of users!

D. Adapt your content to each platform

Although many productivity apps and tools allow you to link your social networking accounts to automatically post the same content to one and the other, we recommend that you avoid these types of solutions.

These social media platforms are all used differently and involve its own content, tailored to its users: You can adapt and atomize your content for reuse on other platforms, as long as you respect the editorial tone of each for maximum success.

E. Use engaging formats

Here's a recent analysis of the Buzzsumo site, made on more than 68 million publications, video content is the format generating the most commitment, followed by images.

Here is the preferred format according to the chosen platform:

Facebook:

- Image or Photo 360
- Video or Lives
- Carousel
- Questions (with GIFs or images)
- Stories

Youtube :

- Videos

Instagram:

- Photo
- Videos on IGTV (less than 10 minutes)
- Insta Stories

Twitter:

- Short texts
- Pictures
- Videos
- Retweet & mentions

Snapchat:

- Stories

Linkedin:

- Photo

- Article sharing

- infographics

Pinterest:

- pins

F. Put yourself in ephemeral content

Ephemeral content is all content on social media programmed to disappear after 24 hours. More specifically, these are stories, introduced by Snapchat and recently popularized more by Instagram, before being taken up again by Facebook.

The main objection to marketers when it comes to ephemeral content is that, in theory, their production may seem like a waste of time. Why take the time to create content that is inherently doomed to disappear after a day?

In fact, it is precisely this urgent aspect that intrigues Internet users and pushes them to look at your stories and to make the suggestions that you offer them.

With the recent integration of Instagram Shopping Stories, this publication format is all the more interesting since it facilitates the access of your subscribers to your catalog of products online.

Use the Stories format to talk about the scenes of your business or your employees, to offer temporary offers and to generate a sense of scarcity and urgency among your subscribers.

G. Take advantage of user-generated content to fuel your social networking strategy

You are not alone in being able to feed your social media content: Internet users can also contribute to fill your pages with publications.

Unlike the content you create, the intention of which is clearly to promote your business, the User Generated Content (or UGC) is created and distributed by the customer (or user), of his own free will.

It can be:

- comments
- Customers' opinion
- Publications on a forum
- Podcasts / Videos
- Pictures
- Blog articles
- Tweets, Facebook posts, etc.

The Facebook contest or Instagram are a particularly effective way to encourage your users to create content for indirectly promoting your brand. This content allows you to access the social circle of your subscribers and put your products forward to find new prospects.

For example, Apple's #shotoniphone campaign, which encouraged people to share photos taken on their iPhones on Instagram, has more than 5 million participants:

USER-GENERATED CONTENT

Such campaigns are very engaging and give you access to a large pool of content that you can reuse in your publications (crediting the source, of course!). Do not hesitate to use it to complement your social networking strategy!

2. Adopt good dissemination practices

A. Plan your publications

Scheduling your publications early and scheduling them for automatic publication can save you a lot of time and make your efforts more effective.

So you can better optimize your Facebook and other publications, align your content with different holidays and important events, and always respect the good publication frequencies:

- Facebook: 1 to 2 times a day
- Youtube: 1 to 2 times a week
- Instagram: 3 to 4 times a week
- Twitter: 3 to 5 times a day
- Snapchat: 7 times a week
- Linkedin: 2 to 3 times a week
- Pinterest: Several times a day

- Hootsuite and Buffer are the popular management platforms that allow you to schedule your publications in advance.

A similar Instagram tool is Later , which also allows you to save hashtags groups and automatically add them to your posts:

Instagram tools for publishing time slots

B. Publish at the right time

The type of content you share and your frequency of publication are not the only factors influenced by your choice of platform ... You will also need to adjust the moments you publish in your social media strategy:

When to publish on Facebook:

From 12h to 15h on Monday, Wednesday, Thursday, and Friday

Between noon and 1 pm on Saturday and Sunday

When to publish on Twitter - B2B:

From 12h to 15h from Monday to Friday, the peak arriving at 15h

When to post on Twitter - B2C:

Before 9am Monday to Friday

At noon and 5 pm Monday to Friday

When to publish on Linkedin:

7:45 am Monday to Thursday

10:45 Monday to Thursday

12:45 pm Monday to Thursday

5:45 pm Monday to Thursday

When to publish on Instagram:

From Tuesday to Friday

Between 11h and 13h

Between 17h and 20h

Of course, these slots reflect averages, but do not apply to all companies in the same way. It is suggested you identify the best social media publishing moments for your industry and target audience to enrich your social media strategy.

For detailed explanations of the procedure, see our article " When to publish on your social media in 2018 ".

C. Use advertising in your social media strategy

Social media ads will be particularly useful to help you discover your products and services to your target audience or to build loyalty among your existing customers.

If you want to include advertising in your social media strategy, our Facebook advertising guides and Instagram advertising will help you optimize your ads to reach your goals faster.

3. Optimize your social media strategy for conversion

A. Use influencers

If you have a very strong social networking strategy, then it is good, you need a little help once in a while to build trust with your prospects.

Influencers are individuals who have achieved a certain level of awareness on social media that are willing to promote businesses to their community.

Today, 75% of Internet users report having already purchased a product following the recommendations of an influencer . And yes! Since it's not about brands but about well-known personalities, influencers are more confident about consumers, especially if they express their opinion about a product or service:

That's why influencer marketing is so useful: it's about building on the reputation of one of these celebrities to make your promotions and boost your conversions. To take advantage of this popularity, you will need to identify the influencers whose community most resembles your persona, get in touch with them through emails or personalized direct messages and negotiate the terms of your collaboration.

Does all this seem intimidating? Do not worry; we've designed, just for you, a comprehensive guide to influencer marketing to help you in this step of your social media strategy.

B. Encourage making contact

Your prospect has discovered you through user-generated content, ads or influencers, and appreciates your quality publications ... What's next?

The next step in your social media strategy: turn your subscribers into customers by encouraging them to get in touch with you on your pages!

To do this, you have several options:

Add calls to action in your publications (call us, write to us ...)

Add a "contact us" button in your Facebook ads

Create chatbots to automatically answer your customers etc.

It is advised you to start by activating messenger on your Facebook page so that your customers can easily join you in private. Here's how to proceed:

Access the settings of your Facebook page

In the left column, click Settings

Scroll down and in the Messages section, click Edit

Select the option "Allow visitors to my Page to contact me privately by displaying the Message button"

Click Save Changes

6. Monitor and improve your performance

If you've taken the time to set your goals, it's good to make sure you reach them! What impact did your efforts have on your visibility, your reputation, your sales.

To find out, pick up your performance indicators and measure them once your social media strategy is deployed:

To analyze your social media profile, use Facebook Insights, Instagram Insights, or Twitter Analytics and determine:

The size of your community

Your organic reach

Your level of commitment

mentions "I like"

comments

shares / retweets

etc.

facebook statistics

To analyze the performance of your Facebook and Instagram ads, use the Facebook Ads Manager and watch for:

Your cost per action (CPA)

Your paid reach

Provided you are interested in the effect of social networking strategy on your traffic and conversions, use Google Analytics and measure:

The volume of social traffic received by your site

The bounce rate of this social traffic

Average time spent on your site by your social traffic

The number of leads collected from social traffic

Take the time to compare your results before and after the start of your social networking strategy and monitor its evolution so that you can adjust your efforts as you go along and maximize your performance.

CHAPTER TWO

FACEBOOK MARKETING 2020

Facebook is the main social network that exists in the world, a network of virtual links, whose main objective is to provide support to produce and share content. It came to expand the possibilities of social relationship and caused a sensitive revolution in the world of communications.

Marketing was no stranger to this change finding in this modality a fertile ground for new concepts and approaches. Facebook is the social network that more users have in the world. There are about 2.2 million users and in it you can find familiar people, participate in interest groups, share content, send and receive messages, make contacts, search, advertise, etc.

Among social networks, it is the one that users choose most often. Facebook is currently the most accessed website in the world. Thanks to its success and great adherence, it is considered as the network that directly influences the politics, culture and public opinion of the users.

But how did that phenomenon begin? What was the trajectory of the founders until today? What are the main resources of this website?

What is Facebook

Facebook is the largest of the social networks : it has 2 billion active users worldwide and turned 14 years old on February 4, 2018. Through this network, you can find familiar people, interact with them, participate in Groups that discuss topics of your interest, share content (images, text, video), send and receive messages, make contacts, search, make announcements, etc.

Therefore, being on Facebook, understanding its operation and the resources it offers is a fundamental step for those who want to expand their business or become known, expand their reach and their digital marketing strategies .

In it, it is possible to create a personal profile or a Fanpage , and interact with other people connected to the site, through the exchange of instant messages, the sharing of content and the famous "likes" in user posts.

In addition to performing these functions, it also allows you to participate in groups according to the interests of people and needs within the social network.

As of today this is the best known forms of connection and is also used to perform quick information searches; In addition to working as a kind of contact centralizer.

CTA marketing on Facebook

HISTORY

The history of the most used social network in the world began in 2003, under the name of Facemash , inside a room at Harvard University.

The site was created by students Mark Zuckerberg, Chris Hughes, Dustin Moskovitz and Brazilian Eduardo Saverin, who were in the second year of the university. With Facemash, it was possible to choose, which were the most attractive girls on campus, from comparison of photos that were collected from the University's security system

It is clear that these types of websites soon aroused the fury of Harvard students and executives, who quickly closed it. At the time, Mark suffered a series of accusations as a violation of privacy and security, facing serious problems at the university.

A short time later, the student began programming the code of a new virtual network with the name of "the facebook", which would later be used, too, by students from other nearby universities.

On this site, it was possible to create virtual friendship ties between university students. And finally, Facebook

The expansion continued, and in the summer of 2005, Facebook was officially opened with its original name, shortly after Mark Zuckerberg's advisor Sean Parker, co-founder of Nepster, suggested the subtle move of the name.

As of 2006, access was released for high school students and also for company workers in general and they were no longer just university students who could benefit from the use of the network.

Soon after, anyone over the age of 13 could connect to Facebook, providing simple information such as name, surname, email, date of birth and gender.

In 2011, the site became the largest photo server in the world. Already at the end of the same year, the number of users who entered Facebook on the cell phone exceeded 350 million.

Today that number is more than double, as well as its unquestionable success and users registered on the network, became 2 billion. Many people stopped using Facebook just as a way to connect with friends and went on to see it as a work tool, as well as a means of disseminating companies and brands .

Social network, the movie

The film that tells the story behind Facebook was critically acclaimed as the best of 2010, receiving several awards, in addition to the Oscar as best adapted screenplay, best edition and best soundtrack.

In it, the trajectory of Mark Zuckerberg is shown, and also the complications that he had to go through since the creation of Facemash.

Zuckerberg appears in the film as a kind of anti-hero, insensitive and calculating, who seems not to care much about the people around him. No one from the Facebook team participated in the film , and, its current CEO, called the script as mere fiction.

Curiosities

With now over 10 years, it is clear that it is already possible to gather a series of curious facts about the social network of one of the most famous CEOs in the world.

Meet some of the most interesting:

1. It is possible to register an heir user of your account

With the option to register the heir user, it is possible to choose a person who will manage your account , in case something happens to you.

The access that this person will have on their profile is limited to the administration of some content, without it being possible to view private information, such as chat conversations, for example.

2. Al Pacino welcoming

When the site still had the name of "thefacebook", when accessing the login page, it was possible to visualize, in the upper screen corner, the face of the actor Al Pacino.

Look:

To this day, there is no justification for why the face of the interpreter of Michael Corleone appeared on the site, but it is known that the image was developed by a colleague from Zuckerberg.

3. The color blue and its relationship with Mark Zuckerberg

Mark has already declared himself colorblind, and for him, the best color is blue. Reason why the CEO decided to introduce the color throughout the site.

4. The languages present

Facebook currently has 70 different language options to be used.

The coolest thing is that, in addition to a wide variety of languages from around the world, there are options such as: "English Upside Down", where everything that is written is upside down.

And that of "English (Pirate)", an English version with pirate idioms, which replaced the "user name" with "pirate name", "Name" is replaced by "Captain's name", "E-mail" it is replaced by "E-bottle" (Something like E-bottle), due to the stories told about the messages sent in bottles.

5. Hackers

In 2014, the number of invasion attempts counted, registered 600 thousand per day. Hackers tried to access important information such as private messages, photos and other user data.

For this reason, it is necessary to generate a password and also activate Facebook's security options, such as providing an access code when entering your account from a device other than yours.

HOW FACEBOOK WORKS

Facebook is basically divided into two worlds - the world of people and the world of business. That is, it offers two profile options to choose from: personal profile or Fanpage.

Personal profile X Fanpage

The personal profile allows you to interact with your friends, post (images, texts, videos), etc. Fanpage, in turn, is the page of your business, it is the presence of your company within Facebook. The main differences between the two options are found in the following table.

Facebook: Personal profile and Fanpage

Type of use: Personal use and Professional use

Users: They are friends and They are followers

Amount of friends: Limited and Unlimited

Who can manage: Single user and multiple users

Customization options: Basic (avatar and cape)and Advanced (avatar, layer, CTA's and plug-ins)

Posts Allows the sending of individual messages and Allows mass message delivery.

Statistics It does not offer any.

- Offers statistics on Facebook Insights.

- It has special tabs.

- Allows advertisements through Facebook Ads.

The type of profile you choose should be associated with your goal when using Facebook. Below, we detail some of the resources presented in the previous table.

Users

If your profile is personal, other Facebook users can be your friends. What does that mean? It means that if you accept another user as a friend or if you accept as a friend of another user, you will automatically follow him and he will also follow you, which means that both can see each other's posts in the News Feed (constantly list updated with the posts of friends, pages and other connections you have created).

Seeing the publication of your friends in the News Feed, Facebook offers the options to react on the post by giving a "like", "I love it", "it saddens me", "it surprises me". Or it also allows you to comment on your friends' posts or share.

In a Fanpage, other Facebook users can be your followers. This is the type of profile that Facebook itself recommends to companies, public figures, etc.

Users who become followers of a Fanpage, receive all their posts in the News Feed and can react and interact with them.

Amount of friends

In the personal profile you can have a maximum of 5 thousand friends. That is, a maximum of 5,000 people can connect to you. And that's because using a personal profile for brand disclosure is against

Facebook's guidelines and terms.

In the Fanpage, the number of followers you can have is unlimited. In addition, the scope of the publications of a Fanpage is much greater. The Fanpage offers resources to boost your posts through an ad, which makes them reach a larger audience.

Customization options

The personalization options of a personal profile are basic: you can customize your cover image, avatar and URL. The possibility of a personal profile to customize your URL is quite recent. This makes the profile easier to find by other users.

The customization options of a Fanpage are multiple. You can describe your page in the "About" tab. A good description is important, so by adding your site address, you can achieve a good search ranking.

You can customize your URL, making it easier to find by other users. One suggestion is: adopt an exclusive and simple name - that will make the search for your page easier, as well as access to it.

You can change the profile picture, cover page and create avatars.

In a Fanpage, you can also create tabs (plug-ins). So, for example, if you want to offer your followers a free Ebook, you can create a tab called "Ebook" and redirect the user to the page where the Ebook is available. This can also provide you with increased traffic on your blog or website .

Another great Facebook customization tool is in the "Preferred audience for the page" tab. This tab allows you to define your target audience. Who do you want to reach? What is the average age and gender of your audience? What are your main interests? In the last tab of the settings, you can define these and other alternatives, so that your page appears mainly for people who fit the profile defined by you.

Statistics

For those who have a Fanpage, Facebook offers some tools that are not available in personal profiles. This is a combo of tools that includes Facebook Insights and Facebook Ads, as well as some special plug-ins.

Facebook Insights is a tool that allows those who have a Fanpage to know in detail the accumulated statistics of the page. You can find out about the reactions to your posts, about the reach of the page, about the visits to the page, about the actions of the followers on the page, about your posts, about your videos and much more.

Facebook Ads is Facebook's own ad platform. Through it it is possible to disseminate not only advertising of your brand, but also content, materials or any other type of post that you find interesting to reach a larger audience.

With it, you can also create segmented campaigns for those who access that social network and also Instagram. It is possible to make hundreds of combinations of public and interests to reach more people.

Facebook, through the resources it offers to those who own Fanpage, is a great tool for business.

Means

Currently, Facebook presents a series of resources that leave the user experience more complete and also more fun.

On top of that, updates on the site are constant, and from time to time, new resources are added.

We separate the main ones:

1. Customization

When you create a personal page on Facebook, it is possible to customize it according to your preferences, adding a profile picture, which allows others to identify you better, and a cover photo.

In case you have a Fanpage, it is possible to use these resources according to your marketing strategy and the visual identity of your brand.

Do you have any difficulty starting a marketing strategy for your company on Facebook? Learn more in this free E-book that we prepare for you.

2. Add friends

It has the possibility to add and connect with your friends and acquaintances, not only from your city, but from all over the world. This became the great key to social networks, since all of them revolve around the relationship between people.

However, remember that only the pages of people have this resource. In the Fanpage, instead of friends, you will have followers who will enjoy your page and interact with your posts.

You never create a personal account to disclose your brand or company. In addition to the fact that your personal page has a limited number of friends that can be added, this action violates Facebook guidelines.

3. Chat

Chat is the quick and practical way to communicate not only with your friends, but with other people who are registered on the network.

In it, it is possible to send messages in real time, in addition to sharing images, videos, links, audios, files and send gifs, figurines and the user's current location.

The resource recalls the MSN instant messaging service, which was gradually replaced by other products such as Skype, social media chats and mobile applications such as WhatsApp, which was purchased by Facebook, in 2014.

4. Follow a page

When you like a page, it is possible to accompany the updates and also the news that is published on it.

The interesting thing about Facebook pages is that they give greater visibility to the owner and allow the public to interact directly through comments, likes and messages.

In addition to that, your personal account shows the pages in a row, indicating what your preferences are. It's an optimal way for other people to know you better, right?

We know well that pages are not the only option that can be followed within the social network. The "like" button has already become a registered trademark and can be used as interaction in publications in general.

Recently, other buttons were incorporated into this option, so that the user can express that he loves a certain publication, or if he felt sad when viewing it.

5. Share content

The possibility of sharing content with other people connected to you is probably the greatest interaction within the website.

By sharing a content, you can share information, news, opinions and news to other users.

It is also possible to share photos, personal or not, directly through Facebook, or through integration with Instagram, which was also bought by Mark in 2012.

In the shared contents, it is still possible to mark friends, show the current location and "add an activity", as something you are seeing, as you are feeling, a cause you are supporting or a book you are reading, just to name a few examples.

Recently, a new resource was also added to the selection of status update options.

It is possible to make a live video stream. That is, it is possible to record something that is happening in real time, and users can interact with you. After finishing, your video will remain in your timeline.

6. Applications

Facebook applications are interaction tools that can be games, jokes and tests that are integrated into your account, even abas (windows that appear just below the cover photo) that can help you in your business, within your page.

And when we talk about abas for Fanpage, the options are countless. They range from the personalization of the same, to the generation of leads, through a Like Gate, which shows different content for those who like and for whom not too.

"Tap" button

The "give a touch" option to someone on the social network was never exactly defined. Facebook introduced it as a way to get someone's attention or simply say "Hello" in a less formal way.

The website itself did not create a specific definition for the function and even, they like to leave the option open to everyone's interpretations.

8. Ads

Through the social network itself, it is possible to create paid ads to attract specific audiences, making it more interesting for people who are watching it.

It is also possible to assemble them according to your needs, in addition to the possibility of boosting your company's sales. The campaigns do not have a maximum value and can be readjusted according to the results and demands that appear over time.

Creation of events and groups

Today, the creation of events on Facebook to announce and invite who you want to go to your party, meeting or meeting became almost mandatory.

This resource facilitates the exchange of information about events and also helps in the control of who will attend. It is also possible to create groups for the most diverse purposes, ranging from gathering people with the same musical taste, for example, to grouping people from the same classroom, so that they can discuss past subjects and activities.

Statistics

Facebook statistics have been growing steeply since its inception, and when we talk about it being the most accessed site in the world, we are not lying!

According to this year's data, the social network has 99 billion monthly active users and 89 billion monthly active mobile users. Secondly, we have WhatsApp and thirdly, Instagram.

For this type of data, that is why companies try to be present in this social network so that they can be seen and so that they can disseminate their own brand.

Why use Facebook as a personal tool

Facebook has both prestige and popularity, coupled with an incredible ease of use, which make it virtually inevitable to have to go through this platform when promoting our personal image. Therefore, if you think of using it for professional purposes, as if it were LinkedIn, you are more than right.

Facebook is ideal for networking allowing you to create groups and events not so formal that will allow you another type of approach. Everything will depend on the imprint you want to give. And not only that, but also, if you want to make radical changes or simply disappear to disconnect a little and change your air, all that is already planned. Facebook is, without a doubt, the social network that most understands the user, in it you will find, in addition to means, a good orientation for emerging problems.

Facebook profile

There are several reasons why many people and companies use the Profile mode and one of them is how you position yourself in front of the audience you intend to reach. The main work we can do with a marketing strategy, using a personal profile on Facebook, is the qualification of leads.

Qualification

Qualifying a lead is, in some way, creating a subtle link that oscillates between the formal and the informal, while there is a minimum of intimacy, we must be careful not to exceed the limits. It will depend a lot on your instinct and intuition and you should never forget that you have to know how to separate the personal from the professional. There are three extremely simple ways to generate and rate leads on Facebook :

Friend requests

Accepting a friend request is synonymous with voluntarily agreeing to receive your messages and view your publications. Of course, much better, still, is when it is the lead who requests your friendship, that can mean an active interest in your proposal. So, either he accepting your request or you accepting his request, in both cases there is an implicit consent that enables you to send content. This consent is the fuel of lead generation . Be careful, do not miss this gesture of trust!

Creating groups you manage

Creating thematic groups is very interesting because it allows you, in addition to creating nutrition flows, to rotate your list of friends. The group mode accepts more than 5000 contacts, therefore, you can create a group and add your friends list, if one day you need to renew it you can delete some contacts from your personal profile, without fear, because they will continue as members of your group.

Once you have put this group into operation, you can create several types of dynamics, both content and segmentation. Promote debates, conduct surveys, create promotions, inform offers, draw a prize, disseminate news and many other ways to keep your audience growing and engaged.

Creating events that you produce

Events are fundamental, they are like the pillars of an intangible construction. We need events to give materiality to our proposal. Without a doubt, you have already seen someone complaining that many people confirmed presence on Facebook, but that very few were. It does not occur to them to think that the error could have been theirs by having an inadequate expectation of a social network and not having used their resources correctly.

Therefore, do not make the same mistake, although it is possible that a facebook event for some unexplained mystery has the same number, or more, of presences than confirmations, in most cases it is not. We generally expect 10% of the confirmations, because the function of the Facebook event is not, in essence, to disseminate, but to stimulate the imaginary in relation to your venture.

TIPS FOR SUCCESSFUL MARKETING STRATEGY ON FACEBOOK

A marketing mix on the Internet does not work without its branch "social networks". Besides, any social network is more effective than Facebook to develop its brand image (brand building in English), its customer relationships and to manage its reputation.

This is due to the significant number of long-range advertising opportunities offered by the social network. You will only enjoy Facebook as a marketing tool if you are correctly exploiting the potential of its possibilities. Find below 8 marketing tips on Facebook that will help you optimize your social media entry and get the most out of this online channel:

1. The basics of Facebook marketing

The basis of success on Facebook is to set up a professional page . This is why it is advisable to take your time to exploit this page as best as possible. All important information must be indicated first. In addition to the location and opening hours, details such as the product palette or the story of the company's creation may be of interest to users.

A fully completed profile containing relevant information in the background gives an impression of seriousness. Images must also convey professionalism and be of good quality. For profile and cover photos, be careful that your images have an ideal resolution and corresponding dimensions.

2. Coordinate all channels

Successful social network marketing

If you want to use Facebook as an element of your online marketing mix, you should harmonize the different channels used with each other to take advantage of synergy effects and incorporate a link to your corporate website.

These referrals generate social signals (social signals) that are considered important for Google and actually constitute a factor for SEO optimization on search engines. Many comments and a high sharing counter reflect the importance and relevance of a site for users, but also for Google.

The managers of the social networks of the company, commonly called community managers, must be careful that all content can be quickly and easily shared and communicate well on the social networks used. The classic actions are as follows:

- Sharing Buttons (Social Plug-ins)

- Buttons to social networks

- Plugin for managing a Facebook page

- RSS feeds and "favorites and bookmarks" services

3. Do not forget the mobiles

In France, the leader in social networks has 31 million active users each month, 25 million of whom have already connected from a smartphone or tablet. In fact, 80% of French users connect from these mobile devices . Around the world according to the same source, 1.6 billion users connect every day in the first quarter of 2016, including 1.4 exclusively from a mobile .

These figures speak for themselves and reflect the importance of mobile optimization . This also applies to social networks, starting with the layout and images. In this regard, Facebook indicates the exact dimensions for profile and cover photos . Mobile users present a low level of attention on Facebook and can thus decide in a few seconds to scroll down when a content does not interest them. All publications must therefore provide concise and relevant images.

4. Increase the engagement of a community of fans

Is the success of a Facebook page measured by its number of likes (or likes in French)? Not really. A "like" only benefits the company if the user is active. Practices that do not comply with the morality of Facebook marketing, such as the purchase of "likes", are to be avoided. Indeed, the acquisition of a large amount of likes does not increase the scope of your publications so far.

The real goal is to acquire fans and encourage them to interact. Fan engagement increases with relevant content. Whoever keeps current trends and those of a community and reacts accordingly, makes sure to gain new fans and increase the range of its page accordingly. A community can develop very quickly with a snowball effect thanks to the sharing and the different contacts of each active fan, who can become interested or clients.

5. Communication and interaction

Having your own Facebook page is ideal for sharing information and news. On the other hand, we should not use this platform only to deliver information, but especially to set up a dialogue and react to the various questions of the interested parties. If you respond to queries with clear added value, you can build customer loyalty and strengthen your relationship with the company.

We get interaction through contests or polls. In addition, polls bring many benefits: by integrating the fans of your page into the decision processYou not only increase the trust they have for the company, but you also gain valuable information about your customers' expectations of the company.

6. The right timing

Good timing

Facebook marketing, by nature, never stops. But thanks to the management tools for existing social networks that allow to post content offline, no employee should stay at his computer permanently. The time aspect, however, plays an important role on Facebook. On the one hand, regularity is important: abandoned pages, on which we have not found new content for years, do not convey an image of seriousness or professionalism. On the other hand, the timing must be fair and a publication should ideally be posted when as many users as possible are connected. Whoever wants to be sure of the numbers can use a tool likeFanpage Karma .

7. Video is the new selfie

Thanks to the introduction of Facebook's new video player (and the automatic play feature), the use of videos on the social platform has become very profitable. Thanks to this, companies quickly gain the attention of their target. Animated images of this kind convey more emotions in communication and they often allow professional representation of products or services. Plus, Facebook is great for spreading viral videos . Two good examples of recent years are the Ice Bucket Challenge or the Harlem Shake.

8. Advertise with Facebook

If you have not managed to naturally get the desired number of fans on your Facebook page, there is still the opportunity to advertise on Facebook . With the help of Facebook-Ads, companies reach their target by showing advertising content in their news feed

HERE'S HOW TO CREATE A POWERFUL FACEBOOK PAGE

Complete the company profile

Go to the "About" section in the left menu and write as much relevant information as you can.

Make sure the contact information (company name, address, phone number) is the same everywhere on social networks. This information must also match those on the company's website.

Name of the page

Make sure the name of your Facebook page matches the name of your company and validate your page to make it the official page of your business.

Category

Add categories relevant to your business area. These categories will allow you to position yourself according to your most important keywords.

username

Create a short representative address so that visitors can easily find your Facebook page. You can as well promote it easily.

Website

Add the address of your website, do not take the risk of losing visitors who want to visit your site or, even worse, lose those who want to buy your products or services.

About

Briefly introduce your organization. Users will be informed about their expectations if they subscribe to your Facebook page. Make sure all your details are complete and up-to-date.

milestones

Tell the story of your company from the perspective of its key moments. By highlighting the most important milestones in your history, you will create a sense of community with your business.

Among the ideas for using milestones, you can post images of your company at the opening, celebrate the good moves of your employees, or promote your product launches.

TIP

OF PRO to attract your most engaged "fans" to your website, add a call to action with a link to your milestones for more information.

Liked pages

Facebook is a place of entertainment, and users who are interested in you want to know what interests you . By loving other pages, you will humanize your business and increase the visibility of your own page and interest in it.

Settings

Allow all your subscribers to post to your Facebook page. You must never forget that Facebook is a social network foremost. It is therefore strongly recommended to leave room for discussion. In addition, a customer comment can tell you a lot about your organization.

To avoid dissatisfaction with users visiting your company's page, make sure to clearly outline the moderation policy that applies to your Facebook page. Tell users what types of behavior or purpose will result in the removal of a message (inciting hatred, verbal abuse, posting sexual content, etc.). Also create text filters to hide specific words that could be found in comments.

TIP OF PRO

Do not delete the publication from an unsatisfied customer. This could especially increase his frustration.

Instead, invite the person to talk to you privately and try to resolve the situation with them. So, not only will you demonstrate the quality of your company's customer service, but you will also avoid the company receiving negative feedback that could hurt its image.

OPTIMIZE POSTS ON YOUR FACEBOOK PAGE

For your Facebook marketing to reach the target, visitors to your business page must provide relevant content for the user. As there are no two users or two identical business pages, it is important to vary your marketing actions on Facebook.

Frequency of publications

Adapt the frequency of your publications according to the type of content and the degree of effort that their production has requested. Consider doing 3 to 5 publications a week, but do not post the same content multiple times.

Do some tests. Try to maximize the clicks and engagement of your target audiences by varying the number of posts per week.

Types of publications

It is very important to vary the type of content you will publish. To achieve this, here is a list, by type of publications, to add to your monthly publication program.

- Make 1 publication linked to your blog;
- Ask your audience 1 question to stimulate discussion;
- Create 1 to 3 non-promotional publications;
- Share 1 to 3 publications related to the content of your brand;
- Share 1 to 3 useful articles from influencers in your industry;
- Publish 1 to 2 videos, depending on your resources. Feel free

to post videos found on the web;

- Take 15 minutes each day to answer questions and comments.

- Observe your results. Then, vary the types based on the publications that brings you the best click through rates and the strongest commitment.

Length of publications

Make publications containing 100 to 500 words. Messages that are too short do not receive the same commitment as those whose content is long enough to give readers the urge to click to find out more.

Hours and days of publications

Know your audience Depending on the family or work situation of your "fans" or any other factor, your best time to post content is likely to vary. Check by trial what are the best days and hours and concentrate your publications in these periods.

Hashtags (#)

Participate in great hashtag -themed web-based discussions or start new ones! This will increase your visibility to the relevant hashtags users who might find you interesting. To learn more about "Hashtags" see our article #Hashtags 101 .

Image quality

Whenever possible, avoid using royalty free images (stock photos). Use original images. Create your own visuals Facebook users prefer the original content.

Make sure, when preparing your marketing strategy on Facebook, to provide time for research and taking photos.

Take advantage of Facebook advertising

Facebook is certainly the most powerful advertising platform to date. Use it to complement your marketing initiatives. Here are the best practices to follow for Facebook advertising

Avoid the button "Put the publication forward"; use Power Editor instead to promote your publications

Avoid-the-button-boost post-put-in-front-marketing-facebook

The reason is simple: this button optimizes your publication for engagement only. Therefore, if the goal of your Facebook ad is to redirect visitors to your website with a publication with a link, you will not be able to optimize it to generate as many clicks as possible.

NB .: See the recent Facebook update that integrates Power Editor into Ads Manager

Install the conversion pixel on your website

Prioritize conversions that bring you revenue. By installing the conversion pixel , you'll benefit from remarketing and optimizing conversions from your ads.

Promote publications that work best

Some of your publications could become viral, and if you are lucky, they will be aligned with your business goals.

If such a thing happens, promote the publication without fail! You will see that it will get a very large reach at low cost. Remember this rule: the quality and interest that people bring to your publication has a high impact on the visibility that Facebook gives it.

Improve the relevance rating of your ads

Follow the relevance index closely. The principle is simple. The higher the relevance rating of your ads, the less expensive your ads will be.

Increase the likes

Increase the likes on your page by inviting users who are interested in the posts you have posted.

Evaluate the performance of your page

The time to want as much as possible as possible is over. Only a minority of your "fans" will see your posts. Remember that the main goal of your Facebook marketing is to increase the turnover of your business.

HERE ARE SOME IDEAS OF PERFORMANCE INDICATORS TO ANALYZE:

Scope, interactions and engagement rate

Follow the scope of your page and the interactions it generates to assess your health. Calculate the engagement rate by dividing the number of interactions by the scope of the page.

Understand the type and timing of the best performing publications. By keeping these indicators in your dashboard, you will learn to satisfy your audiences and improve the performance of your page.

Clicks to your website and conversions

For the majority of companies, the website is a potentially effective tool for earning income, but only if you know how to use it well.

To make the most of your site, it is important that you increase the number of visits and that those from Facebook complement the actions you want to see accomplished. Start by setting up conversions for your website using the Facebook conversion pixel or Google Analytics goals .

google analytics dashboard

Then, evaluate which types of posts bring you the most clicks and the most conversions.

Action button

Assign a value to clicks on the action button. Here's how to evaluate the value of the action button.

Take the example of a call button. Calculate the total value of sales by phone. Divide this amount by the number of calls. Then multiply the result by the number of clicks on the button.

Number of emails acquired

By tracking your website, evaluate the performance of your Facebook page in terms of acquired contacts. An email will allow you to directly contact your potential customers and target more precisely your Facebook ads.

Sales

Of course, calculating Facebook sales directly is the best way to evaluate the performance of your page. This requires a somewhat more complex configuration. Feel free to call an agency if you want to do a thorough analysis of your sales from the Web and Facebook marketing.

Do not forget that Facebook marketing has benefits that are not limited to direct sales. Do not be too quick to condemn a Facebook page that does not seem to bring you the anticipated income.

FACEBOOK MARKETING: GUIDE TO GET CUSTOMERS AND SALES WITH A SMALL BUSINESS

Who doesn't have Facebook today? Look around and look for that "weirdo" that does not yet use this social network (it will cost you to find it).

With that huge volume of users, there is also a huge volume of potential customers. Many businesses are already taking advantage of the platform to grow, get an intimate relationship with their followers and sell.

1 Facebook for startup businesses: it all starts with a fan page

Using Facebook for small businesses means having an already defined content strategy, the first step for a business is to set up a Fan Page (fan page) because this is the type of page Facebook recommends for business.

On the one hand you will have your profile for the private management of your contacts, but for everything that is your business the correct step is to set up a Fan page . Doing so is very easy: you can directly visit Facebook Pages and there you can register a page.

You will have to design two images:

Main image: it is the image that will appear when someone searches for the page and the highlighted one that your business will represent on Facebook. A size of 180 × 180 px is ideal for this image.

Cover Image: this will be the picture that will feature at the top of your Fan Page. It's great to do ads, redirect traffic, or get exposure to a specific subject. The perfect size is 851 x 315 px.

My recommendation is that you put a picture of yourself in the main image and explain how to contact you in your blog or in other places where you can be present through the cover.

2 The landing page

When people arrive at a wall where there are many comments, many contents, they are a little lost and do not know very well what they have to do.

Instead of bringing the new views directly to the wall - people who are not yet your fan - you can also create a Landing page and mark it as the default page.

In this case, the visits of people who are not your fans will end on your Landing page, a page specifically designed for the user to become a fan before starting a relationship with your online presence on Facebook.

To set up your landing page you can use an application called Static HTML tab and that allows you to develop a professional presence on Facebook. Through this totally free application you can define two views: a first view for people who are not Fan and another for people who are Fan.

#3 What content should you use on Facebook?

Basically, the first thing you need to do is mention new posts you wrote on your blog. Do it manually, generate your own posts a few days a week, based on how you've described the blog's editorial calendar.

You can also ask questions (there is a feature called Questions) which is very useful for your fans to get reviews on.

They can also share photos, videos and this is very useful for all physical companies such as restaurants, stores, but also for B2B (business to business) businesses. For example, it occurs to me that presenting a printing press ' digital machines can be very valuable, in photos or on video.

Most businesses are not making ample use of these tools that are actually useful and allow us to offer a glimpse of what's behind, what companies are selling and that's very optimistic.

You should share links and I recommend that you not only post your own links, but also that if an article has been written in a journal that you think is worth highlighting for people following you... Do it, don't just share your resources!

Attempt not to be very formal, so don't frighten the friends. Be human, talk about things personal and amusing. In short, be no pain.

How many times you have to do it each day?

Those you want. You usually realize that the more active you are on Facebook, the greater the benefit you usually get to this network. Nor is it about becoming a spammer: everything depends on your ability to add value (I usually do it twice a day at the most).

Very often, when I look at small business ventures on Twitter, the topic of the post is the one that sins the most. They're having difficult time letting go and not writing like in a sales brochure.

It's just about sustaining a professional relationship that continues for ever. Chat with one of your customers when you drink a coffee or eat. That client has become a friend over time and you don't always talk about work with friends, right?

Any more nothing less. See how easy that is? We continue to develop your future plan on Facebook with this exclusive Facebook guide for small businesses.

What tools can I use to easily and quickly create the content?

Non-designers are given numerous designer tools. Many software that will help you create content without having to expend too much time or completing a complete Photoshop course.

These are recommended:

- Canva : the best known tool for creating content for any social network. Enter, register and you can create the cover, profile picture, Facebook Ads ads and publications by dragging photos and editing text.

- Pablo : Do you just want a nice phrase and a nice background? Try Pablo, Buffer's quintessential tool for creating more content.

- PicMonkey: collages, filters, photo edits and all that is needed for photos.

- Recite : if you don't like Pablo's photos, Recite is your choice. Write a quote or phrase and choose from the numerous templates to create your phrases in seconds.

#4 How to get more engagement on your Fan Page Another very interesting business resource is Facebook Ads, an online advertising platform in which you have two types of commodities: one is traditional advertising and the other is sponsored.

Both goods have the idea of making your own Fan page or external website available and aim to get more fans or link to a landing page that you've made. Facebook ads is fairly cheap, and has an exceptionally good segmentation capability.

You can segment on geographical location criteria, socioeconomic level, sex, topics of interest, you can segment by "Friends of your fans," you can do a lot of things and I really recommend, if you are a small business, launch a 5 or 10 euro campaign a day (you can control the budget you spend) because it can bring a lot of value to your business.

Ok, if you're a solo entrepreneur, think about Facebook ads so you can expand within this social network in your "distance." For example, developing a Landing page would be an interesting strategy, where you are offering to register your newsletter, a document or a mini-course.

In this scenario, depending on the subscribers who subscribe to your Facebook newsletter, you can track the impact of your promotion on Facebook, which helps you to set a cost per subscription that is a very useful measure for tracking, more interesting That cost per click on your ad.

#5 You spend money with the idea of growing your database of potential clients on an online advertising campaign. An opportunity rather than a cost, yet another case in favor of keeping a small business operation on Facebook Where can I view my Facebook statistics?

Facebook Insigths is Google Analytics counterpart but within Facebook. It's your page's analytics section and it's interesting to know a little about the stuff that's going on there: see the most popular posts Learn a little more about the user profile that connects with your content Learn how new users hit your landing page or wall See which sites they visit Know what external connections get you more clicks and more fans Anyway, a sequence

Like any boss, to make your decisions, you need the details. Facebook Insights is your unique, small business Facebook scorecard.

#6 Expand Social Widgets on Facebook These social Facebook widgets virtually serve to illustrate the behavior you can have on Facebook in your blog. There are several types of widgets: one of them is the "Like" button, recently completed with an option to send to the user group of Facebook.

These two buttons are very valuable and we recommend that you integrate them into your blog so that users can easily share content.

Another popular widget is an activity feed that displays the face of a blog follower and invites non-fans to page fans.

As you can see, the conversation is added to the conversation. If you introduce these resources on your blog, your audience can grow on Facebook as well as on Facebook. People prefer to read content directly on Facebook. Facebook is a time-consuming platform.

Think about these resources that Facebook offers for free and integrate social information into your blog.

The third widget I want to comment on is the Facebook comment thread. This allows you to leave comments on posts you publish on your blog, but you can use your Facebook profile directly.

With this plugin, conversation threads are developed through comments made on Facebook. This is very positive and a very good alternative to spam in comments.

There is a re-effect of the conversation between your blog and Facebook. This is a positive effect. Please try to use it.

7 advanced use on Facebook

One is the use of the Facebook application. If you have the money to invest and have a good idea, developing your own application for Facebook is a great way to gain business visibility and become more accessible. fan. The application needs to know that it can access a lot of profile data for users who are fans of this application. You can also know more data about the users who use it.

Of course, this has significant development and integration costs, but it also has great business value.

I think it's suitable for many businesses, not freelancers or people who start alone or have just launched a business, but for a restaurant for example, integrating an application to reserve tables can be of great interest or that people share their cocktails Favorites with the bar where they will spend time.

8 Turn your fans into subscribers

A Facebook fan is somewhat volatile. He is just one step away from keeping in touch with you, and even your fans can only see 7% of your posts.

Isn't it a very sad statistic?

For this reason, try to collect as much traffic as possible from your Facebook page to your blog or website. Then you need to make your fan a subscriber by email. This way, you can always contact your fans the way you want.

9 Throw yourself now

You don't need anything else to start working with Facebook. Follow these steps and your community will gradually grows around the page. You will bring in more confidence and your followers and clients will feel you as a more intimate company.

And if you like this Facebook marketing guide for small businesses, I will ask you in return.

Just never pass it to the competition.

HOW TO MAKE MONEY ON FACEBOOK PAGE

With more than 1 billion users, Facebook is a great opportunity for businesses that want to use Facebook as a sales or advertising tool. But the question that many people ask is is it possible to generate income on this social network without having a company?

Is there a way to start making money on the Facebook page if I don't have a business? There is no way: there are 5 different ways to do it! Requirements for monetizing Facebook pages

The first essential requirement is clearly having a Facebook page. Several readers have asked if they can make money with their Facebook profile. And the answer is yes.

However, since personal profiles are not specific, it is much more difficult to monetize personal profiles than Facebook pages. Your Facebook profile can include friends with completely different interests. Some people like techno music, others like rock and pop.

Some people have pets, others don't like animals. On the other hand, Facebook pages are more specific because fans have the same common interest.

When creating a page about rock music, only those who like rock music click "Like". If your page is aimed at pet owners, only people with dogs, cats, or parakeets will be fans of it.

So the first thing to keep in mind is that you need to have your own Facebook page. Forget to make money using your personal profile on this social network. Remember that you can now create ads on Facebook.

1. Make money on Facebook with mentions

If you have a lot of fans following a Facebook page publication, you can make money by mentioning or promoting your company, company, or anyone who wants to know you.

Many small businesses, brands, or even entrepreneurs don't exist on Facebook or have their own pages, and they want to increase visibility among users. That's why they pay pages to many fans featured in Facebook posts (with photos) to attract customers and increase visits to web pages.

To achieve this type of collaboration, you can search for Facebook or Google companies interested in your page, create the most relevant lists, contact them, and reach an economic agreement in exchange for publication Is the best.

But be careful: do not contact anyone. You need to do it with companies and brands related to Facebook page themes and interests. If you have a mobile phone page, it's not logical to mention a food company, for example. Ideally, contact a brand that sells accessories and products related to mobile phones.

2. Sell your own products

One of the easiest ways to make money on Facebook pages is to sell your own digital products. These include e-books you write, such as e-books, guides and manuals, online courses you create, articles that you can download immediately as mp3 music.

To sell them, simply upload these files to a mega or other storage platform and post an attractive photo with a brief description and payment link on Facebook. If you repeat frequently on Facebook pages, fans should feel free to saturate with ads, so don't look into this type of post. It is recommended that you publish one of these promotional posts for every 10 regular posts.

3. Promote affiliate products on the page

Do you have your own product? Then you sell other people's items and receive a commission for every sale you get. This is called "affiliate marketing".

This method works exactly the same as the previous method. Instead of adding a link to the product, you need to publish the affiliate link provided by the registered company.

There are many companies that have affiliate programs: Clickbank, Amazon, Apple, Zalando, Asos. Search the Internet for the best company for Facebook pages, sign up for its affiliate program, and select products related to your fans. Publish an affiliate link and receive a total commission each time someone clicks on that link and buys a product.

CHAPTER THREE

INSTAGRAM MARKETING 2020

Defining an Instagram marketing strategy is the first step for anyone who wants to use this network to promote a company or even their personal brand. With the growth of this network in Brazil, many brands have been looking for Instagram as an alternative for the promotion of their products and services.

Fashion, food, beauty and tourism, for example, are sectors that can not be left out of Instagram , because they are the "face" of this network and therefore, find in it a great place to get leads.

The big problem is that many of these brands are moving to Instagram marketing , still in an amateurish, makeshift fashion. In a market as competitive as social media marketing , treating a corporate Instagram account the same way you treat your personal account is a true strategic suicide.

It is therefore important that the brand first of all prepare itself by devising a marketing strategy on Instagram , before going around publishing anything and praying for some result. We all know that this does not work.

- Understanding the concept
- Understanding Instagram Marketing
- Determining Your Instagram Goals
- Content Development

- Structure preparation

- Alignment with other strategies

- Results monitoring

- You will find that this basic planning of a digital marketing strategy on Instagram is not as difficult as it may seem, but it is certainly critical for the brand to achieve good results.

The walkthrough for crafting an Instagram marketing strategy

Below you will see the step by step to work out a digital marketing strategy on Instagram and design your company, or personal brand in this tool.

1 - Understanding the concept

The first step in building an Instagram marketing strategy is to understand the very concept of social media marketing, which has very different characteristics from other digital marketing strategies.

Social media marketing is relationship-based, meaning you first build rapport with your followers and fans, and then subtly present your business proposition. So this is a medium strategy and so you need to start now and then reap the rewards later. There is no immediate result in social media marketing.

2 - Understanding Instagram Marketing

The marketing on Instagram, whether personal or corporate, subject to its own rules and understand these rules and network characteristics is essential to your marketing strategy.

Instagram is by definition an entertainment medium. Therefore, your business approach should be to display, that is, to be in the right place for the right people, without interfering with the natural conversation of the network.

3 - Determine Your Instagram Goals

As with any other social media platform, when designing an Instagram marketing strategy you must clearly determine what your main goals are with your brand presence on this channel.

The marketing on Instagram does not work or works very little in some situations, such as direct selling, for example. Therefore, your proposal should be to create an alternative to your other online marketing strategies.

By clearly determining your goals, you will be able to select your metrics and make a really technical measurement of the results. It is not for any other reason that in our Instagram Course , we put this issue right between the first training modules.

4 - Develop exclusive content for Instagram

Another interesting feature of Instagram is that it is extremely demanding in terms of content. In our social media marketing course , I always say that content is the main tool in this area, and Instagram would be no different.

A marketing strategy on Instagram differs greatly from people using the tool. While in private use, we do not have much concern with the sequence of actions, in the case of corporate use, everything needs to be thought of.

This is why it is important that you study the posts of companies in your area that stand out on Instagram to understand your competition and also to see how your audience reacts to these posts.

Images - Always work with unique and innovative images. No need to go around taking beaten images to put in your publications, because they don't work, just because they are already "part of the landscape".

Texts - Invest heavily in creating interaction-generating text, with thought-provoking link baits and strong call-to-action, so that your posts can achieve their goal of building rapport with their followers.

Hastags - Hashtags play a major role within an Instagram marketing strategy, so create your own to achieve greater reach and also monitor the most popular hastags.

Content is largely responsible for interactions on Instagram, so believing that the brand can succeed in this area without proper care in pre-preparing this content is a waste of time.

5 - Prepare your structure

Instagram, even more so than other social media like Facebook and Twitter, is a conversation environment, so you will need to have an interaction structure, otherwise all your efforts to create an Instagram marketing strategy will be wasted.

People comment and ask questions in your publications, and it is very important for you to create the relationship ties we mentioned in the first item of this article that you are ready to interact with these comments and questions.

The person responsible for these interactions will need to be fully aligned with the Instagram Marketing strategy designed by your team, otherwise the conversion potential of these interactions may be lost, or worse the brand may end up in a social media crisis

6 - Align your Instagram marketing strategy with Facebook's

We all know that Facebook is fully integrated with Instagram, so it makes perfect sense to align your Instagram marketing strategy with your Facebook marketing strategy to create a digital marketing synergy between them.

Not that you will replicate everything you do on Instagram, in the Facebook interface, which would be a big mistake, but to make these two tools interact with each other, aiming to enhance each one of them.

7 - Set up a good monitoring system

There is only one way for you to analyze the success of an Instagram marketing strategy, as with any other type of online campaign: Building a good conversion tracking strategy.

One of the major problems with Instagram is precisely the lack of links in paid publications, they are only allowed in ads. As a result, most Google Analytics- based traffic monitoring techniques, such as UTM Tagging, are greatly compromised.

Therefore, you will need to create a differentiated tracking system through specific Landing Pages sent in response to your interactions so you can track incoming leads generated on Instagram in your conversion funnel.

HOW TO CUSTOMIZE YOUR INSTAGRAM?

KEY ELEMENTS ON YOUR PROFILE

Have you opened an Instagram account? You can immediately take care of a very simple thing, even before starting to post your first photos: customize your profile.

This is often one of the first elements that will see potential subscribers, so it plays a key role to make a good impression. But how to customize his Instagram ? In this article, I will tell you about the five essential elements to inform for the first impression to be positive!

Overview of an Instagram Profile

If you look at an Instagram profile , you will find that it is composed as follows:

Instagram profile: 5 important elements

INSTAGRAM PROFILE: 5 IMPORTANT ELEMENTS

1. There is a user name . It is thanks to this name that other members of Instagram will be able to mention you, it is also the name which will appear in the URL of your profile. For example, I am @salutbyebyeblogwhen I am mentioned and https://www.instagram.com/salutbyebyeblog/when I quote the URL of the profile.

2. There is also a profile picture , most of the time a logo, a picture of the person who manages the account or a photo symbolizing the main theme of the account.

3. Then there is the name of the account (separate from the username): it is a name a little more marketing, which we see in particular in the search results Instagram.

4. The fourth important element is the Instagram bio , some lines of biography to put forward your account.

5. The last element is the link you include in your Instagram profile, which will be clickable.

Business accounts have a few additional options, which I will return to at the end of this article.

These elements can be modified by clicking on the button "Modify the profile", which gives access to this screen on mobile:

Edit Instagram Profile

EDIT INSTAGRAM PROFILE

1. Your username

This is one of the first things you have to choose to customize your Instagram.

If you have a website, be aware that the rules for choosing an Instagram user name which amounts to also choosing a domain name.

A name that does not have spaces

A name which, ideally, does not contain characters too complex to memorize (points, underscores, useless numbers, doubled letters as in "elisabeeeeth" ...).

A name that takes your "brand" if you have a blog or you are present on several social networks, It makes memorizing easier.

A name that can be up to 30 characters while knowing that it is better not to fully exploit this limit and opt for a shorter name

And if the username is already taken

You can use a tool like Namechk to see at a glance if a name is available on Instagram as a domain name and on different social networks.

This is also the most common problem encountered: the Instagram user name you would like is already taken. More frustrating still, it is sometimes used by an inactive account, which seems to be abandoned.

To date, Instagram does not offer a miracle solution: it simply advises you to choose a variant of the username you have in mind.

The alternative is to contact yourself the profile you want to retrieve the name: by private courier, by e-mail if the person provides a contact address in the bio of his profile, or by a third party site (search on Google the name of the Instagram profile, the person may have mentioned it on a blog or other site that it manages).

If it is an inactive account, chances are you will receive no response. It may also happen that you are asked for a sum of money in exchange for the release of the desired username: it is up to you to assess whether it is worth it, and to assess the risk of a scam (nothing prevents the person from taking the money without releasing the account later).

Instagram

Even in the case of brands, Instagram remains quite protective vis-à-vis its users. If someone uses a name that is a registered trademark , you can not necessarily get it back. You have to prove that the person is using your brand in a misleading way that could mislead members of the social network.

If this is your case, go to this page , choose "I have a question about usernames" then "My request is for a business account" and then "This username is used by someone else and I can see its content when I access the web address "and finally" I wish to report an infringement of my trademark ".

Change or change the user name

The username can be changed along the way, remember it is a pretty heavy decision: indeed, the username will change where it appears on the Instagram app itself (mentions, comments, etc) but there will be no redirection of links posted to your profile outside the network (ex: websites that mention your account).

You can customize the Instagram username by clicking "Edit Profile" at the "User Name" line. The change is instantaneous.

Get a verified badge on Instagram

Some accounts have a small "Verified Account" blue badge next to their name. It is a badge attributed by Instagram to public figures, celebrities or well-known brands, which attests that this is their official account and not an impostor, as here in the official account of the Game Of Thrones series :

Verified account with blue badge on Instagram

VERIFIED ACCOUNT WITH BLUE BADGE ON INSTAGRAM

A known personality or brand can make a verification request by going to the "Settings" menu of Instagram, then in "Account" and finally in " Request verification" . All you will give is a proof of identity (official ID if you are a natural person, tax return or statute if you are a company).

Instagram verification request

INSTAGRAM VERIFICATION REQUEST

2. Customize your Instagram with a profile picture

The Instagram profile photo is an important part of your identity: it is displayed on your profile, in 110 × 110 pixels format in general. It is preferable, for a good quality display, to put it online in a higher resolution (at least 180 × 180 pixels).

You can choose a nice portrait of you, your logo or an image that perfectly embodies the theme of your account. If you are present on several social networks, it is often relevant to use the same visual everywhere to be more recognizable.

If your logo does not fit in a square, nothing prevents you from choosing only its graphic part , without text, if it is sufficiently recognizable ... Nespresso thus content with the "N" instead of the full brand name.

Nespresso on Instagram

NESPRESSO ON INSTAGRAM

We can also opt for a more compact version of the logo , as do Galeries Lafayette, which transforms their complete logo into a sober "GL" on Instagram, while respecting their graphic identity.

Galeries Lafayette on Instagram

GALERIES LAFAYETTE ON INSTAGRAM

It is often quite relevant to have a profile picture consistent with the general tone of the Instagram account (for example, applying the same type of settings if it's a photo).

3. The name of the Instagram account

As I told you at the beginning of the article, this is the name "marketing" of your account. It will appear on your profile, of course, but also in the Instagram search results if your account has the opportunity to appear there ... It must not exceed 30 characters.

Instagram Search Results

INSTAGRAM SEARCH RESULTS

Initially, I made the mistake of repeating the name of my blog alone ... but in reality, it is advisable to use this space to include keywords relevant to your theme, much like you would on the homepage of a website, in the title tag , in a referencing perspective .

We can either do it in addition to its brand name (which is repeated twice, in the username and in the account name), or completely get rid of the brand name and post only a name descriptive account .

This is the example of the Petit Bison children's decoration brand, with an explicit account name, "Children's Deco".

Little Bison on Instagram

LITTLE BISON ON INSTAGRAM

4. Customize your Instagram bio

The Instagram biography is just a few lines of text, which has the power to attract the attention of a passing visitor! 150 characters to exploit at best to convince!

The idea of the bio Instagram is above all to explain what you offer on your account. Who are you and why would you suddenly decide to follow you?

You can use hashtags (which will be clickable) and emojis . However, e-mail addresses and URLs will not be clickable even if you can add more. Feel free to skip lines to make your message clearer and readable.

A good bio Instagram shows your personality while explaining what you do. It can consist of a few sentences to deliver a complete message ... but also a few points in the form of a list if you share unrelated information.

The Instagram biography can for example include ...

What you offer (type of content, products, theme, activity);

Where you are

One way to contact you

Practical information (eg for a shop, specify where you deliver);

Another account that is important to you (second Instagram account, YouTube profile, etc);

A call to action (download an application, visit a blog, use a specific hashtag to share photos, etc.).

Emojis can be used wisely to save space in your biography: for example, use a flag to indicate your location instead of writing "Location: France"; use an envelope to highlight your contact information, etc.

Here is for example the bio Instagram account "A piece of cake" which offers high-end pastries. At a glance, you can find all the information you need to know : the activity; a contact address; a way to find out more; the places of delivery; the identity of the two pastry chefs who count.

Instagram account A piece of cake

INSTAGRAM ACCOUNT A PIECE OF CAKE

5. The Instagram profile link

At the bottom of the biography, Instagram allows you to add a URL. This is the only place on the social network as I write where the URL is clickable.

So you can use this space ... knowing that you do not have to include a link to your site's homepage at all. You can for example ...

Put the URL of your last article (we can modify the URL as often as necessary, so many bloggers choose to add their most recent content).

Put the URL of your news of the moment (for example, a new collection in the case of a fashion brand).

Put a URL type Linktree : it is a URL that will refer to a dedicated page, with a menu to access all your important content. That's what Galeries Lafayette do, and here's their Linktree page:

Linktree for Instagram

LINKTREE FOR INSTAGRAM

Put a URL to a landing page dedicated to your Instagram followers on your blog.

Put a URL to creative content: your last YouTube video for example.

Put a URL to an action that is important to you: for example, a newsletter sign-up page, a donation page if you have an association or project to support, etc.

I advise you to use an "explicit" link rather than a non - personalized code link, like zoup.la/ezr439zea5. It makes you want to click when we know (roughly) where we will arrive! Also check that the page you are referring to appears on mobile ... because even if there is a desktop version of Instagram, the site is primarily used on smartphone.

Do not forget also an important element: your URL will be displayed just below your biography. It means that you can use the last line of the Instagram bio to encourage action on your link, put it in context.

And also for business accounts

To customize your Instagram when you have a business account, you have additional options, accessible by clicking on the button "Edit profile".

The Instagram category

It is visible only on the application, not on the desktop version of the site. It allows to indicate to which sector you belong , thus avoiding to repeat it in the bio Instagram itself.

Among these categories, there are either typologies of profiles (for example "Personal Blog", "Cruiser", "Local Company"), or themes ("Travel and Transportation", "Sports and Recreation" for example).

Communication options

As a professional, you can include contact information about your business: e-mail address, phone number, business address. This can also free space in your biography because these coordinates will be displayed directly on your profile as a call-to-action .

A call-to-action contact on Instagram

A CALL-TO-ACTION CONTACT ON INSTAGRAM

A call-to-action

Since we are talking about call-to-action, beyond the contact information, Instagram offers you, in the menu "Communication Options" after clicking on "Edit profile", to display an action button .

This time, it is a button related to different booking services (Appointments by Facebook, Eventbrite, OpenTable, TheFork, Yelp, etc.).

Customize your Instagram account to get started

When you come to customize your Instagram through these key elements , we already put all the chances on his side to deliver a clear message to people who will fall on the profile.

TIPS TO GETTING FOLLOWERS ON INSTAGRAM

Since Instagram has been acquired by Facebook, it is increasingly difficult to develop an account because the social network has implemented an algorithm that reduces the visibility of publications. But there are "good practices" that, in my opinion, will never be harmful!

Win Subscribers on Instagram: Classic Rules of the Social Network First, there is a simple principle on Instagram as on other social networks: to win subscribers, you need to get interested in the network. Okay, really get involved. I note that often, because of lack of time (or because of laziness, it has to be admitted), I just like the images that fly before my eyes without actually making an effort to write a comment, to go in search of new accounts...

However, it is indeed when one is involved that one derives the most advantages in terms of visibility!

As a social network, Instagram receives the same types of advice as other networks: carefully complete your biography and choose a profile picture; do not flood subscribers with low value added photos; take advantage of the social functions of the network: be interested in others while respecting the ethical principles that we know well (sincerity, no advertising of the type' I follow' Some use the network just to share their daily lives with friends and family (and often have private accounts where they only accept those they know), others-this is my case-also use them to uncover talented artists, to imagine in front of stunning locations, to search decorative ideas...

Tips that work to get more followers on Instagram Original and insightful content Instagram remains a network of "beautiful images." It can be blamed for fostering a cult of excellence, but most of the accounts that grow rapidly and well are those that post quality content.

These are cool pictures, not usually shot with the last but still well framed SLR, not blurred...

A story to tell, I also think, after a few years spent on this network, that people appreciate hearing a unique and personal "voice" behind a (beautiful) image.

Share an anecdote, a life scene, some stories to feed his account, to get a little cold out of the "picture book." It's not easy to keep a certain discretion, but I'm sure it works.

Make your account known that Instagram is a network at the heart of your digital life. And in order to have more followers, you have to give it a place: promote your Instagram account on your blog (through an icon or by embedding any images in your articles), relay your Instagram photos on your Facebook page, build connections between the sites that you run so that we know the presence of your account, include your account in your newsletter...

Nothing also prevents you from pressing your account more explicitly, by posting a message on your blog or on another network to encourage people to join you on Instagram. This year, I did it 2 or 3 times and it helped me to win a couple of dozens of subscribers.

Exploit hashtags and geolocation According to a 2015 report by Dan Zarrella, analyzing nearly 1.5 million Instagram photos, adding hashtags on his pictures raises both the number of likes and the number of comments. Like Twitter, hashtags make it easy to find all the photos related to the same theme.

I discovered very recently that the practice I used was detrimental to my account: like many people, I don't want to "parasitize" the legend of my photo by posting 25 hashtags! And I decided to share in a comment my list of hashtags. Today, I have the impression that I gain more subscribers by limiting myself to a few hashtags and integrating them directly into the legend of the photo.

After several months of stagnating with the same number of followers, this helped my account to start winning again.

You can also allow the geolocation of your images. As a result, they will be more easily linked to a specific location when a person searches for information on the place in question (city, restaurant, trade, etc.), an additional way to gain visibility.

Use Instagram filters According to another Yahoo Labs / Georgia Tech study, filter-based photos are 21 percent more likely to be viewed and 45 percent more likely to receive comments than filter-free photos. According to the report, "the rise in contrast and brightness has a favorable effect on the number of views and comments." The same is true with retouching, which raises the temperature of the object by making it colder.

On the other hand, rising exposure appears to have a negative, though slight, effect on the opinions, even though it is positive for the comments. This goes back to Dan Zarrella's claim that low-saturation images earned 598 percent more than brightly colored pictures! In the same way, the bright photos collected 592 percent more like the dark photos.

At the end of the day, members of the social network choose filters or retouching that enhance the picture without distorting the filters that turn the image. We remain at this level in the search for authenticity.

For my part, I no longer use the filters offered by Instagram, I prefer to manually change some settings (especially contrast / sharpness) to improve the rendering of my photos... But I'm avoiding the heavy editing that's too much of the original photo.

Chat with your subscribers

This is a point on which I still lack investment, recognize it :) If I think to like the comments that I receive or to answer with a small message when the commentary allows, there is one thing that I do little and works well on Instagram: work well your legends !

Photo captions provide a unique opportunity to share trivia, ask questions to your subscribers, tell stories. It creates a link and it's effective for engaging in a discussion.

As on a blog, we can test different things: short legends, long legends, ask a question, explicitly encourage subscribers to comment (according to Dan Zarrella, this explicit dimension would promote interactions).

Keep a coherence

Again, this is not always an easy point to respect ... but for the subscribers (or members of the network who discover you) find it there, it is better that your account releases a certain coherence , that it is in the contents that you post, in your interactions with your subscribers, in your publication frequency.

As on a blog, there is not necessarily an ideal publication frequency but many studies suggest posting several times a week to increase its commitment.

Post at the right time

Instagram no longer displays photos chronologically but highlights posts based on what you are likely to like. Nevertheless, the timing is important because the commitment you receive from the publication plays a lot on the visibility that the social network will give your photo (same on Facebook for me!).

Try to find out when your community is present : rather the evening after dinner, the morning before going to work, on the lunch break, during regular business hours? It can vary from one community to another, which is why I am always dubious when a study announces "ideal publication times"

HOW TO CREATE AN INSTAGRAM MARKETING STRATEGY FOR YOUR BUSINESS

Today, visuals have never been more numerous - be it a quick selfie of our lunch date or the latest video of our pet doing an amazing trick.

This increase in visual content flooding social networks is therefore even more pronounced on Instagram .

As a result, several brands are integrating Instagram into their strategy for growing their business. Videos, gifts and photos generate high engagement rates. If Instagram has become so important, it's because it creates a global social network by connecting people only through visuals, making it a powerful way to capture and hold people's attention.

In recent years, marketers and brands have been trying to capitalize on this monumental growth of Instagram. It has been proven that promoting your business on Instagram is a daunting tool if you learn the tricks to sell your brand on Instagram.

Instagram not only allows you to connect with people and gain visibility, but also paves the way for your brand to be recognized and trusted by Instagram users.

Here are some statistics that show that Instagram is a powerful platform for brand loyalty:

• In 2017, about 70.7% of all US businesses are on Instagram. That's almost twice as much as in 2016 (48.8%), and this was largely influenced by the inclusion of Instagram profiles in the business.

• 65% of all top performing Instagram posts involve products. Despite the fact that it's not good to promote yourself every time, Instagram users like to look at product photos from time to time. In fact, photos / videos of celebrities / influencers (29%) and lifestyle photos / videos (43%) are behind product images and videos.

• 7 out of 10 hashtags are tagged on Instagram. Hashtags not only help social media users to classify and organize content, but they have also played a key role in creating some of the most successful marketing campaigns.

You must now leverage this client source and use Instagram marketing to grow your business. To sponsor content on Instagram, you must have a Facebook page and use a corporate Instagram profile. Once these two preliminary operations are completed, you must configure your form, define its budget and finally publish it. Here are the steps to follow to create your strategy.

1: Start with a compelling Instagram Profile

Your Instagram professional profile should in no way resemble your personal Instagram account. And it is better that "you" rarely (if at all) appear on this Instagram page.

Here's how you can create a compelling Instagram profile that will help you improve your online presence to attract more customers:

biography screen instagram

A. Use an attractive bio

Experts also believe that an Instagram bio should prompt a customer to take action while highlighting the personality of the company.

Bio must be both interesting and informative. You should be able to hook your followers. You need to be convinced that adding Instagram users to Instagram will improve the content and value of your feed.

Provide details related to your business in a concise and relevant way. This should appeal to the Instagram community you are targeting and should also reflect the tone of your shared images. Also discover how to post multiple links in your Instagram bio.

B. Link to your site

Only Instagram bios can place clickable links, so please enjoy. A link to the site is shown in the space just below the description (at the top of the Instagram page).

Including links to websites is important to Instagram's marketing strategy. Make sure that the URL is readable, not a series of random characters. Also find a way to post multiple links to your Instagram bio.

Create an Instagram marketing strategy # 2: Build an Instagram aesthetic stream

Product images make a huge contribution to online shopping. Make Instagram your showcase to multiply this power.

Nearly 67% of all consumers rely on the product image before making their purchase decision and give them a higher priority than evaluations or product information.

Feel free to enhance your brand aesthetically while showing off your products.

biography screen instagram 2

A. Enhance your brand identity

You must be able to value the brand identity of your business. Most of the aesthetics of your Instagram feed will be based on the identity of your company. It's up to you to give the tone and the personality that you want to send back in the posted content.

B. Do not compromise. Focus on the target marke

Respond to your target audience without compromising on your brand identity. Please note that the Instagram feed is aimed primarily at current and potential customers. Find out what in your product or brand is most appealing to your target audience. And reflect that in the posted Instagram content.

C. Stay consistent

Your business will only gain brand identity if you remain recognizable. Make sure your Instagram profile image is consistent. Add the thumbnail of your profile picture to all your Instagram commitments and engagements

D. Find your competitors' strategies

Study the content of your competitors and get an idea of what they are promoting on Instagram and essential to get into your market. Do they use user-generated content for their products or services? What kind of content do they post to Instagram? How often ? What is their hashtag strategy ?

Get new information on what competitors are doing and new ways to improve your own marketing strategy.

Create an Instagram marketing strategy # 3: Be creative with your Instagram captions

Creative Instagram legends are one of the keys to attracting new customers, but it's not easy to find the right description for your image.

post jcrew instagram

A. Spend some time

Many users feel compelled to post images just after taking them. Instead of rushing, you need to take the time to properly define the caption of your image to captivate your audience. Your results will only be better.

B. Short but effective

Instead of unnecessarily stretching the legend, make it short but enjoyable. Remember, users will probably spend only a few seconds displaying your photo before moving on to the next one, make your text quality over quantity, through the description use your creativity to make the image more attractive. Do not be cold, but talk as you would outside the networks, it should boost your commitment. Instagram users hate formalities.

Create an Instagram Marketing Strategy # 4: Use Strategic Hashtags

Hashtags are used on Instagram to allow users to follow the content they are looking for. You should use hashtags strategically so that more users can find your posts during the search.

Here are some practices to help you get the most out of hashtags:

- Use less than 15 hashtags in each message.

- Select some frequently searched hashtags.

- Integrate hashtags that are only relevant to your target audience: reactions may be fewer, but more qualitative.

- In case of a brand specific hashtag, create hashtags that are branded.

- To make sure your brand in a local area, use location-based hashtags.

If you would like more information on the use and choice of your hashtags, click here.

Create an Instagram marketing strategy # 5: Create compelling stories on Instagram

Instagram has its most popular feature to be the Stories (400 million daily active users from June 2018). If you can relate stories to your brand identity, they will automatically connect you emotionally to your audience and add meaning to the content you post.

The stories you post contribute significantly to creating brand loyalty. Instagram offers you the best platform to post storieswhich gives credibility to the brand. But at the same time, your Instagram feed should reflect the purpose and image of your business (and your brand), as long as they create consistency. Random and disconnected content can be confusing. So be careful what you are about to publish.

Create an Instagram Marketing Strategy # 6: Develop a Committed Community

Since feeds on Instagram change quickly, it is likely that your content will be buried in no time. The only way to change this is to add hashtags to your posts on Instagram.

In fact, hashtags have an important role to play in placing your business in different communities on Instagram and are linked by a keyword, which will allow you to find your posts as long as Instagram is operational.

In addition, you can also consider inviting Instagram ambassadors to share your product / brand on their feeds. Creating a group of ambassadors to spread the benefits of your brand to their subscribers will help you reach and win more customers. Encouraging Instagram followers to post reviews and photos will also help you reach many other Instagram users.

Nearly 78% of all consumers buy products / services based on a brand's social media. As a result, the more people you have to share and promote your brand, the more likely you are to convince potential customers to buy your product.

Another great way to create an engaged community on Instagram is to share the marked photos of your subscribers on your Instagram profile, adding the content of your users to your own Instagram feeds will create a good feeling, which will then be associated with the brand you promote - 65% of Instagram users believe that when a brand talks about them, they feel happy and honored.

Get off the beaten path! Feel free to try new things. The Instagram algorithm changes constantly every half hour. So, everything that worked for you last week may not work for you the next week.

Therefore, it is best to continue experimenting with new ideas all the time. If they work well keep them, otherwise, try something new. Be original.

However, you can not avoid elements such as your brand content, high-quality images, user-generated content, engaging and engaging publications, and hot topics. The tips mentioned above will surely help you set up the best Instagram strategy.

HOW TO OPTIMIZE ACCOUNT AND SELL

How to optimize and sell an Instagram account?

If you already downloaded the application to your smartphone and got your Facebook account as registration data, or if you generated new credentials to access your new profile, stop here and see how to optimize please.

Basics about Instagram accounts

What everyone doesn't know when they decide to follow a sales strategy with a presence on Instagram is that this social network was originally designed to share images, and text has a place.

This doesn't mean it's impossible to implement a sales strategy on Instagram, but in that case you need to know tricks and practices to attract traffic that not everyone knows .

For example, to attract traffic to a website or a specific URL, you must do the following:

See the highlighted links you have in bios in your publication so that your followers can visit it.

Be sure to use the Instagram links correctly because you use dedicated

use #hashtags mostly to indicate your brands to increase visibility and reach more people.

Share a mini video introducing news on the website.

Unleash your imagination and share a clickable Instagram story that hooks the community from the start.

Instagram offers many possibilities for optimization and content creation in various formats, but you should be aware of the following restrictions:

Characters: The career limit is 29-150, but you can write a maximum of 2,200 for comments and text accompanying a post.

Tags: You cannot tag more than 20 people per post.

Hashtag: Up to 30 per post (never from a third party).

Follow-up: 200 follow and unfollow per hour.

Comments: 60 per hour.

Like: I like 100 other posts per hour.

Automation: Until very recently, this was not possible with external tools. Well, you may schedule publications from some of the most famous tools such as Hootsuite and SocialFlow in a somewhat less restrictive way.

Need some tips for Triunfagramers who want to sell on Instagram? Then write down:

Tag people you don't know or comment and like using an automated application! Please respect the restrictions that may cause you to lose your Instagram account labeled as a spammer.

Do not abuse the hashtag of each publication. Also, do not combine this practice with including additional comments.

Never forcibly get followers in a short time, like buying followers or following / unfollowing.

HOW DOES THE INSTAGRAM ALGORITHM WORK

There is no doubt that with the passage of time and especially from the relevance that Instagram took in this 2018, the publications do not have the scope that was previously available.

This is nothing new, it happened with Facebook several times. Precisely because of the changes in its algorithm.

Thus, it is important to know how the Instagram Algorithm works, in order to try to do things well and therefore increase the visibility of your account.

Currently the Instagram Algorithm is focused on certain key points, which we will see later:

- The engagement of your community.
- The interaction with your followers.
- The speed of interaction.
- The duration of the visualizations.
- The relevant hashtag.
- Do not act like a robot.
- Others.

Why is it important to know the Instagram Algorithm?

Knowing how the Instagram algorithm works has a direct impact on the visibility of your account.

This is simple, even if you do one or two things well, if you want to grow your account or your competition has better results, it is probably due to this factor.

If you have a business account or want to improve your personal account, I always suggest analyzing the competition.

In short, you have to know your competition and know how to master the Instagram algorithm, in order to grow and increase your visibility in this social network.

The Instagram feed versus the Instagram timeline

Something I want to remind you before you start talking about the Instagram algorithm, is that you have to understand the difference between a feed and a timeline.

What is an Instagram feed?

The Instagram feed is the list of posts that appear within your account. Basically your publications in chronological order.

What is an Instagram timeline?

Instead the Instagram timeline, are the posts you see, when you enter the Instagram application.

You must learn to master the Instagram algorithm, in order to make your posts more visible on the timeline, beyond how beautiful, orderly or cool your feed is.

HOW TO BEAT THE INSTAGRAM ALGORITHM

Now, we are going to see recommendations based on the new Instagram algorithm , in order to overcome it and increase the visibility of your account.

1 - Increase engagement

The first thing you should know is that Instagram rewards publications that have a high dose of interaction (or engagement).

This means that Instagram takes into account the amount of likes, comments, views on videos, saved and others.

When you receive comments and I like in your posts that likes the algorithm of Instagram and therefore is a good sign for it

For example, a great way to increase engagement is that apart from uploading posts to your Instagram feed, take advantage of Instagram

Stories since the algorithm also takes into account the interactions in them.

2 - Interact with your followers

It doesn't matter if you have a comment or hundreds of them, you should interact with the people who interact with your posts.

This is another factor that the Instagram algorithm likes.

There is not much to say here. You have to worry about interacting and generating as many conversations as possible. That means that publication is being a success.

3 - The frequency of your posts

Instagram growth algorithm

Following the tips to master the Instagram algorithm , there is the issue of how often you make posts.

It's really about finding a balance.

Neither exaggerate making dozens of publications a day, nor spend days or weeks without publishing anything.

Look at it this way, the less time you spend updating your Instagram feed, you will have less interactions and therefore, your visibility will begin to decrease.

4 - The speed of interactions

This is somewhat complicated to achieve and has to do with affinity.

Imagine you have an accident, call 3 of your friends. One arrives in 5 minutes, another arrives in 6 hours and the other arrives in 3 days.

Which of your friends has more affinity with you?

Exactly, the first.

This is how affinity works on the Instagram algorithm. The faster the interactions of your followers with you, the better, because it means there is greater affinity.

How to achieve this?

Ideally, maintain a good relationship with your followers, interact often with them and most important of all, publish in the hours you know that most of your Instagram audience is connected.

5 - The duration of the visualizations.

Surely you did not imagine this, but the Instagram algorithm takes into account the time people spend viewing your post.

It's crazy not?

Obviously here you will have to use all your creativity to make people, while reviewing their Instagram timeline, stop to see your posts in detail.

So always think of having content that really makes people stop to look at it.

6 - Know your best times to post

My best schedules according to the Metricool planner

There is not much to say here.

If you want to increase your interaction rate, increase affinity and thus dominate the Instagram algorithm, you should know the best times to publish.

Some important questions you should ask are:

Who are my best followers?

Who interacts more with me?

What areas or countries are these people from?

What time are they most active?

What days of the week are they most active?

7 - The relevant hashtag

While the instagram algorithm penalizes excess hashtags (Shadowban), it also favors those publications that use relevant hashtags.

This means that before putting 15 or 20 hashtags to your posts, maybe with less than 5, but they are relevant, you can increase the visibility of your account.

So remember to analyze well what Instagram hashtags work best and don't forget not to overdo it, but above all, they are relevant.

TIP: Save different groups of hashtags relevant for different occasions in your smartphone's notebook. For example 4 or 5 hashtags for "dinners" or maybe for "party" or for "holidays"

8 - Post Instagram Stories or use IGTV

This is simple.

If Instagram brings out a new functionality, then you should take advantage of it because it surely affects the algorithm.

At the beginning Instagram was only for posting images. Then Instagram Stories joined and now there is Instagram TV (IGTV)

What does this mean?

What if you use Instagram Stories and also IGTV, you will surely like the algorithm and reward you with greater exposure.

9 -Don't act like a robot

Did you ever notice weird comments in your posts? Comments that simply have an emoji or a phrase like "good image" and nothing else?

It is very likely that they are Instagram bots.

Usually these Instagram bots are configured to follow certain accounts, follow certain hashtags and even comment with phrases that are predefined and are always short, with some emoji and may even be irrelevant to the publication.

Well, don't do the same.

For example, if all the comments of your followers, simply respond with a "Thank you" and a happy face, it is likely that over time the Instagram algorithm believes that you are a bot.

Be original, answer the comments, vary the phrases, generate conversation.

Don't be a meat and bone bot.

10 - Make Live Videos

Since 2017 Instagram allows you to make live videos, however, many of the accounts I follow do not usually use this feature.

If you want to grow on Instagram and beat the algorithm remember what I said before, you should take advantage of the functions of this social network.

Include in your Instagram strategy, publish live videos every so often.

Apart is a great way to interact with your followers.

11 - Take advantage of Trends

No, I do not mean that you join any challenge on the Internet, nor that you put aside your strategy to take advantage of a trend that has nothing to do with your account, brand or person.

But there are always trends that can be exploited.

Usually the trends are loaded with many topics of content, hashtags and even ways of communicating.

Take advantage of trends, are key to increase engagement and interactions at certain times.

12 - The use of Instagram features.

Finally, my last advice has to do with something I commented on several points.

If you want to master the Instagram algorithm, then it is key that you use all the functions that this social network has or leave.

It is simple, if Instagram launches a new functionality, it is very likely that its algorithm privileges those users who are early adopters, use them and even make them fashionable.

Before arriving late, my advice is to arrive early and take advantage of this new functionality, to boost your visibility.

MONETIZING YOUR INSTAGRAM PAGE

How to make money with Instagram: ways to monetize your account

1. Influencer marketing

Most users hate advertising and this is leading us to become more reluctant to direct and cold marketing actions.

It is clear that everyone who has a product or service needs to sell.

"Nobody likes to be sold, but everyone likes to buy!"

If you have a blog, you will know that the advertising banners make you lose credibility and that is why, in recent years, the influencer figure has become stronger and with greater conversion when it comes to promoting a certain product or service.

If you aspire to become an influencer thanks to Instagram , know that you don't need to be famous or have the measurements of a model.

What is now valued much more is the level of engagement , that is, the loyalty of the followers.

An example of this is Diana Miaus who has started collaborating with brands when she had only 20 thousand followers.

She, for example, is what dominates a micro-influencer , since it has a smaller community than others but at the same time very faithful to its contents.

At this point you could ask me: Serena, how can I become a micro-influencer?

Think about what you like, your passion, what you spend a lot of time.

Create a special relationship with your followers and do not become obsessed in the number of them, as in your level of engagement.

Simply put, interact with your followers to the fullest and build a solid and faithful relationship .

To do this, I recommend you also read these two articles:

13 most common mistakes you can't make on Instagram

How to use Instagram stories to grow your account

Once you have obtained a small community, you can register with these platforms to close your first collaborations:

- Tapinfluence
- Influenz
- The Mobile Media Lab
- SocialPubli
- Coobis
- Twync
- BrandBacker
- The shelf

You have to register and some of them not only ask for your Instagram account but also your blog and other social networks.

How to find collaborations on your own

There are many companies that still do not understand the potential of Instagram and why they should use this social network.

There are others who don't even have an account and don't even know what Instagram is.

So, what to do?

To avoid wasting time and not falling apart, I recommend that you focus on companies that already understand the potential of Instagram.

To do this, you can see what your "competition" does and see who they close collaborations with.

What I do is enter an account similar to mine, look at the post and see if there are particular mentions.

If the account in question has a blog, this information is usually found in «Contact», Media Kit or in the «Collaborations» section.

Once the first companies have been identified, I recommend you create a document where you can name them or better, create some notes on your mobile to remember them.

In this way, in a couple of weeks you can create your database with these potential accounts.

It will be much easier to start with companies with which they have already collaborated than to jump into the void.

2. Affiliate Marketing

If you have a blog, you'll know what I'm talking about.

If you do not have it, affiliate marketing means when you promote a product or service of another person and they pay you a percentage for each sale made.

On Instagram you can do it in two ways:

1. You can put the affiliate link in your BIO

2. Create a story, explain the product / service and add the link

There are many companies you can work with, such as:

Amazon Affiliates

Skyscanner

Airbnb

Tradedoubler

To shorten the link, customize it and track it, I recommend using bittly.com .

Also, if you want to better understand how this system works, I advise you to read this article by Frank de Lifestyle al Cuadrado : The mega guide of Affiliate Marketing.

3. Shout4shout

It is one of the methods that I have spoken to you in the Instagram guide and that many accounts use to grow quickly.

It consists of mentioning another account (for example in Instagram stories) and in turn, the other account does the same with yours.

This will make you known among his followers and the possibility of getting new followers in a very short time

If it is done with a great account, you will have many followers, likes and click on the link of your BIO.

There are also accounts that, to grow rapidly, are willing to pay for this type of collaboration.

In fact, if you have a page with millions of followers, you could charge about $ 40 - $ 200 for s4s (shout4shout).

Now think.

If you manage to sell a shou4shout a day, you could earn interesting money by spending a few minutes of your day.

Interesting right?

That's how young American Tim de @gentlemensmafia got rich .

His accounts have millions of followers and he created a network to exchange payment shout4shout.

But be careful, everything that glitters is not gold.

For a Shout4Shout to really work, you have to be careful:

to. Do not promote anything that is not typical of your niche

Do not forget that your followers follow you because they are interested in your page. If you propose something different, that does not fit with your niche, you could lose them.

b. Do not accept all kinds of offers

If the photo you are asked to promote does not convince you, do not do it.

4. Sell your photos

Although it is not as easy as it seems, there are people who earn money selling their photos.

As you can imagine, if you are a professional photographer, Instagram is the perfect showcase to publicize your works of art.

And these are some of the platforms where you can sell your photos:

Foap

Twenty20

5. Instagram as a source of traffic

People who ask me how to monetize their account always answer the same thing.

If you want to make real money with Instagram, the most common is that this social network is a source of traffic for your online business.

It is best to build a business that goes far beyond Instagram.

How?

For example, creating a blog or a web page , writing a guide or creating an email list.

If you get your followers to go to your sales page or your blog, you could get a lot of traffic.

Therefore, social media experts and marketers advise creating an Instagram page as a source of traffic for your blog and your e-commerce.

Instagram has great potential compared to other social networks such as Facebook.

Above all Instagram is free and if you want to invest money, ads are cheaper.

Then, engagement on Instagram is much higher than on Facebook.

Have you stopped to look at how many likes your last FB post has? And in IG?

6. Sell your Instagram account

If you have many accounts, you can create a true network.

And if one day you get tired of Instagram or want to leave this world, you can choose to sell your account, so that someone else uses it without having to start from scratch.

Where to sell it?

fame swap

viral accounts

CHAPTER FOUR

YOUTUBE MARKETING 2020

Over the years, YouTube became synonymous with opportunities to put your brand in evidence , because it is possible that you appear before your audience and that you have close relationships with content that stimulates interactivity.

Seeing that it is the most popular video platform in the world and the second most used search site on the planet, being present there is crucial for your company. On the other hand, YouTube is directly linked to Google, which can contribute to improve the positioning of your site in web searches.

Set up your study

If you want to make videos and spread them online, you need to have a good planning and invest in some particularities, such as the quality of your materials. Today, with so much content available on the internet, it is important to make investments so you can offer some quality.

Data behind the YouTube monster

- There are more than one billion users

- Every day hundreds of millions of hours are seen and billions of reproductions are generated

- 300 hours of video are uploaded every minute

- 50% of the reproductions are from mobiles

- Youtube is available in 75 countries and in 61 languages

- There are more than 1 million advertisers (most are small businesses

YouTube video marketing work is increasingly essential for a successful strategy. In the end, the contents of this type have a high potential to transmit information and contribute to the dissemination of products and services.

Although the content is the king on the web, it is very important that you worry about the most technical aspects, such as a study, which is one of the most appropriate solutions to help you save money with production and also have more dynamic processes and less bureaucratic

Then, before worrying about the equipment and all other things, the first step is to find a suitable place to set up the studio to record your videos, in order to meet your needs in terms of structure and equipment.

The space

Remember that the studio needs to have enough space for you to record your videos, for the equipment, the actors and the technical team. A place that is small can be very bad for the quality of the videos produced and also cause some kind of accident, since the production equipment is fragile and can be easily damaged.

Acoustics

Always look for places that are as distant as possible from noise. Always privileges the isolation of any type of sound that may hinder the recording.

Another recommendation to protect you from noise is through investments in expanded polystyrene plates or foams, which can be placed on windows and doors. On the other hand, egg maps are also efficient to make the acoustics of the environment better and you can place them above the foams.

Lighting and colors

If you were to use a closed room as a study, you should invest in lighting. Therefore, never forget that a poorly lit or shadowy scene can make your production ruined.

So, if you cannot count on natural light, which is very difficult, pay attention to illuminate the environment in the best possible way.

Another issue that needs attention is about the color of the environment you will use. In the end, depending on the paint and the color used on the wall, the light can be reflected with color and make your whole scene look bad.

Therefore, you should give preference to opaque paints, which absorb light instead of reflecting it. On the other hand, if you use a wall layer as the background of the images, choose the most neutral colors that do not cause much interference, in case they are reflected on products or people.

White ends up being an excellent option and, in case you want, you can always decorate the walls with paintings, clocks or elements that have to do with the content. If you have technical knowledge and want to produce more professional videos, it is worth investing in a chroma-key.

Finally, it is worth remembering that you must take care of the organization of the stage as a whole, that is, always have a beautiful and clean environment. This will bring a lot of credibility to the videos and will ensure you a number of subscribers on YouTube and, consequently, a participatory and connected audience.

Equipment Choice

The quality of videos is one of the essential factors for you to succeed in the YouTube strategy The good news is that there are investments for all budgets. You can record with a more solid camera and even with your smartphone.

It is important to invest in audio quality and good lighting, which will make a leap in the quality of your recordings. Next, we will highlight some equipment for image, audio and lighting. Look!

Image

When opting for cameras, there are numerous models and prices. Regardless of whether you choose a smartphone, a webcam or a more compact camera, what is really worth is the budget. Then, study the possibilities:

tight budget : in case you have a cell phone with a good camera, preferably in Full HD, you will know that you have material that has advanced technology. A problem with the cell phone is the few focus adjustment options, but it is perfectly possible to record excellent videos for YouTube with the phone, duly attached to a tripod;

medium budget : the most compact cameras, depending on the model, are worse than many more recent cell phones. Because of that, it is very important that you pay attention and choose those that have a value similar to the input DSLR cameras;

Looser budget : DSLR cameras are the best bets for you to have optimal video quality. If you want something more practical, bet on that type of camera. But there are some simpler models within that category, such as the Canon T5 and Nikon D3200.

Audio

Audio is very important for recording quality videos. In the case of camera audio, it ends up being damaged by the environment, so the microphone ends up being necessary. In that case, pay attention to the possibilities:

tight budget : your smartphone probably has a microphone embedded in the hearing aid. It is not the most perfect scenario, but you can record your voice separately on the cell phone that way. Thus, you hide the hearing aid in the shirt and hold the microphone in the neck. The sound may not be so perfect, but it will probably be cleaner than the camera sound.

Medium budget : you have the option of investing in a lapel microphone with a connector that is serious in the smartphone. Recording with a lapel microphone, the sound quality of your video will be much better and your audio will be clear to your audience.

Looser budget: in case you record alone, invest in a lapel microphone and a digital recorder. You can find some kit options with good recorder microphones. Unquestionably, the result will be much better.

illumination

Good lighting is also essential to get your viewers to follow your videos from beginning to end. Although natural light works perfectly for different videos, you can also invest in some types of equipment, such as a panel of LED lights , which can be installed directly on the camera.

Although you can make more solid investments, as in the LimoStudio kit, which creates light and diffuse Illuminations, or in a Neewer

Camera, a ring light, which is circular and can be installed in the camera.

Use YouTube video techniques in your favor

So that the work you present on YouTube has an excellent level of quality, you can use some filming techniques, which are essential to do a differentiated and successful work. Below, we highlight recommendations that may be indispensable for your strategy. Let's go to them:

- lighting: a well-lit video is vital for your content to be viewed in a completely comfortable way by the viewers, since it prevents data, information and some places from being hidden;

- animations: animations offer endless possibilities for you to create your videos. They give dynamism to your content and can be another attraction for people to really be attentive to your ideas;

- narration: some more complex concepts can become a very difficult task to express. Therefore, a more personal narrative can make all the difference when explaining some ideas;

- music: choosing a music that transmits the desired emotions is an excellent way to give strength to the contents of the videos ;

- humor: using humor is another way of fixing the public's attention in a general way, but you must do that in a very timely manner and avoid excessive informality;

- graphics: listing the fruits on the performance of a company in the course of the video can become somewhat boring, but through the use of infographics it is possible to make the understanding of information easier, in addition to avoiding reading the numbers;

- emotion: telling exciting stories are great ways to pass the company's message to the public and can make the connection with customers established. On the other hand, it is worth remembering that exciting videos sell more;

- Duration: choosing how long a video will last is a very important technique, since it is essential to find a balance between the speed in which ideas are expressed and the period in which the user will be attentive to the video;

- colors and filters: using colors and image filters is essential to give more depth to the messages and these can be used both in more comparative videos, as in others with more educational character;

Company history: telling a brief history of the company and its processes so far is an essential technique to value all the progress achieved. On the other hand, it reinforces the identity and image of the brand.

Success in the type of content

Ensure you use content that is really relevant to your audience . The contents must really solve the problems of your audience and to help you in this task we will highlight 10 content ideas for YouTube. Look!

1. Explanatory videos

People really like video tutorials, in which things are explained in detail . Making videos that clarify people's doubts is a great way to have many views and participation.

2. Promotional videos

It is necessary to pay attention to the promotions of products and services that your audience has interest. Based on this, you can create content for some promotions you are doing. Remember that everyone likes a promotion and you can exploit that strategy in a timely manner.

3. Vlogs

People love to know details of the racks in people's lives. Therefore, if it were something that suits your business, you can make more informal videos, telling about content you learned, events you participated, among other issues.

4. Recommendations

People like to receive recommendations of all types. Therefore, if you have any ideas or are experts in some subjects, make videos indicating ideas that will certainly help your audience.

5. Make webinars

Webinars are live videos in which you can give a class or a dissertation. Its duration usually varies and depends a lot on the subject and the type of audience you want to reach. It is an excellent way to establish closer relationships with potential consumers and create your authority in the market.

Audio Marketing: the evolution of content

Undoubtedly, audio is the type of multimedia that can best adapt to the routine: even with the existence of other content distribution formats, it lost its importance.

Read more "

6. Product Reviews

The product review is one of the video ideas that generate the most views. Nowadays, many people go to the internet to know details of a product and that can be an excellent idea to spread your merchandise and promote your brand.

7. Customer stories

You can promote some videos by telling success stories of some clients. Remember that people connect more easily with other people than with brands.

8. Videos on how to do

Many people go to the internet to solve their problems. From the moment you create videos teaching people to do things, you will naturally build a good audience .

9. Personal videos

People like to know about experiences. Therefore, if you have any interesting personal history that refers to the professional context, you can exploit that in the videos and generate very identification with your audience.

10. Motivational videos

Motivational videos are also an excellent idea for you to identify with your audience and make him participate with your brand.

Configure the YouTube channel

In case you have finished creating a YouTube channel, we will give you essential recommendations for you to stand out. Follow, below, some channel configuration recommendations:

1. Add channel art and profile picture

It is very important that you add an art for the channel and a profile picture to have a visual identity that is easily recognized by your audience. For the profile (or avatar), it is interesting that you have a logo and for the art (or cover photo) you can use images that establish a synergy of your work with what you will address in your channel.

2. Add a description and the client of your other digital platforms

To describe your business, it is interesting to tell a little about your story and your proposal on YouTube . It is worth presenting, for example, your mission, vision and values. It is also an excellent opportunity to add links from other platforms, such as Facebook, Instagram and Twitter. For that, you need to go to the settings and enable the option "Customize the layout of your channel".

3. Upload videos

To upload a video on YouTube, you just need to click on the arrow icon, which is at the top edge, to the right of the screen . Next, the tab will appear to upload the video. You have the option to select several videos or, if not, you can upload one at a time.

An important recommendation is that, at the time of uploading, you should place the videos in the private option. That way, you can edit it before it is released to the public. After having everything correct, you can put the video as public.

4. Understand the differences between public, unlisted and private

On YouTube, there is a possibility that you configure the privacy of videos. There are three options and each of them has some peculiarities:

Private: When you select this option, videos cannot be viewed by the channel owner. It is recommended to place it in private when the video is not yet finished or when you wish that no one else has access to its content;

Not listed: through this option, your video can only be seen by the people you want, that is, the general public will not be able to access. In that case, the channel owner sends the video link to the people he wants to see.

Public: This option allows the video to be open on your channel and viewed by anyone who searches.

Create a check-list

To be successful with your YouTube video strategy, it is very interesting that you have a check-list to highlight all the steps of your videos. In the first moment, you can check your steps in four situations:

1. Preproduction

At this stage, you need to be aware of issues such as duration, format, quantity of videos and content management . Here, it is also the ideal time for you to write a video script, fully aligned with the needs and motivations of your audience.

2. Production

After deciding what will be done and produced, the ideal is to implement the content strategy defined in the previous item. Some content corrections will also be made, because many times what was put on paper is not very good in the video . On the other hand, in this stage the care related to the place of the recording, the formats and the angles also correspond so that everything goes perfectly.

3. Post production

After recording a video according to the planning of the previous stages, it is necessary to learn how to edit videos, in order to correct the possible imperfections that are in the content. At this stage, the entire video must be evaluated before being released by means of opinion tests between the teams and the management of the company.

4. Disclosure

This is one of the most important stages for professionals involved in the video marketing strategy for YouTube. After all, remember that, with good content in hand, the possibilities of a video are unlimited.

In this case, it is worth the disclosure on the site itself in social networks in e-mail marketing, so that you guarantee the effective opening rate and, mainly, a greater conversion in relation to other types of format.

In addition to evaluating each of these stages, it is essential that you are attentive to the SEO strategy for YouTube, so that your video can appear well positioned on Google. To stand out, it is necessary to invest in the following techniques:

- always use keywords in the title;
- know all the tools of Youtube and learn how to exploit them;
- effectively describe your video and learn to use tags;
- share it on social networks, sites and wherever you can;
- use calls for action (CTAs) in videos.

STEPS TO CREATE YOUR YOUTUBE CHANNEL

But I don't roll up anymore and let's get to the important thing. I will explain how to create your own YouTube channel in just 5 steps ! And if you don't believe me ... you just have to keep reading.

We start!

Step 1: Sign in with your Google account

Firstly, log in with your Google account. This step is essential, because without logging into Google you will not be able to create it.

Step 2: Go to the YouTube page

For now you cannot tell me that this is being complicated, since you have only had to do a few clicks! And if you think that the thing is going to start getting complicated, you are wrong, because creating your YouTube channel is going to be eating and singing. I assure.

The next thing you have to do is visit the YouTube page . Once there, at the top right you will find your icon or photo, depending on the data you have completed in your Google account.

Click on it and choose the option «My channel» . If even with the explanation you are still a little confused, look at the image below, in it I show you where to click. So don't panic!

Step 3: Choose the name of your channel

This is where the interesting begins, and the really important thing for your YouTube channel . It is at this moment, when doubts assail you and when suddenly a thousand questions come to your head.

Think about the name of your YouTube channel when you create it!

For all that and because I am very nice, I have added a section where I give you my best advice when choosing a name for your channel.

How to choose the name of your YouTube channel?

The name of your channel is very important and before launching to put any one I recommend that you think carefully. Do not forget that it will be the first thing users see and it will be directly related to the searches they do. There is nothing!

So remember:

The name must be related to the theme of the channel or the name of your brand.

Use shorter names

Do not use symbols, signs, dashes or numbers.

If you don't have a lot of imagination or you can't think of any name for your channel, I recommend you use tools that help you generate names, such as Business Name Generator.

At the end of the whole, when you are filling in the different fields on the YouTube page, you will see the option Use a company name or another name?. I want to explain the difference:

With a personal account you can only have a single YouTube channel associated with your account.

If you use a brand channel, you can have multiple channels associated with your account. These channels are also known as brand accounts. You can also add additional administrators and owners to your brand account and manage your channel together with your collaborators or teammates without the need to share passwords.

I would recommend this last option. But you have the last word.

Step 4: Customize your channel

Here you must customize your channel. That is, you must associate it with your brand image. To do this, use the colors and corporate images of your company or business.

Keep in mind that the design of your channel is essential to make a good first impression to your followers, so do not skimp on time.

Your followers, know them well!

And above all, take care of the details, this will make your YouTube channel make a difference with respect to others of similar content, or with respect to your competition.

Advice, complete all the required information, be original and above all make use of quality images.

Completing the channel information and using good quality images will not only help you gain followers. If not, which also will help your channel to like the YouTube algorithm more. That is, all advantages!

So, so that you are not lazy or lazy, I leave you a small guide where you can and complete the information with quality!

Channel Icon

Channel Icon will be your sign of identity. Therefore, you must choose a quality image and according to the channel you are creating.

For example, if it is a company, the right thing is to use your company logo. If it is a personal channel, I recommend the logo of your personal brand, or a photo that is associated with you.

Channel header or banner

The header is the largest image of your entire channel, so think well that you will show on it.

Choose a perfect cover that reflects your spirit or that of your brand. When designing it, you must take into account the different formats depending on the devices from which it will be displayed (smartphone, tablet, desktop computer, etc.).

Therefore you must ensure that the most relevant is seen from all devices, that is, that it is located in what is known as a safe area. And how can you know? Well, very simple:

When you upload the image, in the preview pop-up, you will see how it looks on each of the devices.

These are the sizes you should use:

YouTube channel icon 800 × 800

Header size for YouTube channel 2580 × 423

How can you create covers for your YouTube channel?

You may not have knowledge or resources to make the header of your YouTube channel. For this reason, I leave here some tools with which you can create original, creative and professional covers.

Best of all, is that with these tools you can also create your own header for your channel in a very fast and simple way.

Canva

Desygner

Crello

If in this process you also need to use royalty - free images with high resolution . I recommend you visit these pages:

Pixabay

Pexels

Unsplash

Complete your channel information

Now, what you have left to do is complete basic aspects of your channel. To do this, I leave some tips:

Make a brief description of your channel . It is a huge necessity to tell the public what they are going to see in your videos.

The location .

You can add an email address so they can contact you if your channel is commercial.

You must also add links to your website or different profiles on social networks.

The above is essential to attract the attention of the public and end up visiting the content of your channel.

You see the difference? Which of the two do you find most attractive ? The answer is more than obvious!

Step 5: Upload your first video

To do this you can click on the link "Upload a video" . You just have to start uploading the file and choose your privacy: public, hidden, private or scheduled.

But what is the difference between hidden and private?

Well, the truth is that these two concepts are very easy to understand. In fact, here I leave the distinction between the two:

Hidden : Hidden videos can only be viewed by those users who have the video link.

Private : A private video can only be seen by the user who uploads it and by the people he chooses.

STEPS TO MONETIZE YOUTUBE VIDEOS

There are several steps we can take to monetize YouTube videos but first of all, you must have your own YouTube channel, that you have generated content of interest and above all that you see that your subscribers are growing. As soon as you see that, you can start on how to monetize the videos you upload with these steps:

AdSense and YouTube

It is probably the best known method also because it is in front of everyone's eyes. Do you know those ads that are seen before and after YouTube videos?

Well, this means that the channel you're visiting adheres to the YouTube partner program and monetizes the channel with AdSense.

What is it?

In practice, every time someone shows an ad, there is a small benefit. The monetization system is based on the CMP, that is, the cost per thousand. That is, the advertiser (who is the one who invests in advertising) pays a total for every thousand people who see your ad.

Youtube in turn divides the income with the youtuber but do not believe that the amount you will earn at the beginning is going to be a lot. It is said that the average in Spain with the program of partners and with the ads is about three euros, but the reality is different and there are many videobloggers who claim to charge just a few cents for each video with integrated ads.

This is due to the many changes that YouTube has made within its partner program in recent years and months specifically. In fact, it was recently announced that YouTube has introduced a new limitation for smaller channels. Thus, from now on, to join the partner and Adsense program, you must have more than 1,000 members and a total of 4,000 hours of "observation time" accumulated during the year. So write this down to start thinking about being from the program, let the ads begin and you can charge for it, no matter how small.

Affiliations

Affiliations are another method used by a YouTuber to make money with YouTube. But what exactly are they? It's very simple: it's about recommending products (or services) and taking a commission every time someone buys that product through the link we put for them to buy.

But as in the previous section, commissions are variable, although it is said that with this second method, the percentage can be up to even 70%, but of course to reach that level you must be a YouTuber with millions of followers and as No, of visualizations.

Influence marketing

Similarly to the previous point, there is also influence marketing. That is, you appear in a video drinking a certain brand drink or wearing the clothes of a particular firm. That is to say, to indirectly advertise in your videos, of brands that pay you for it.

Sell own products and services

Here a real world opens up. For what reason? Because the possibilities become virtually endless. Depending on our type of channel, we can offer connected services or create ad hoc products.

It is nothing new for a YouTuber with a certain popularity or fame, to end up publishing a book, take out his line of clothes, make-up or also launch a new product. Without a doubt, if you have millions of followers, it will allow you to earn a lot of money, but it is still an expansion of "business" to which only those who already have a certain weight in the YouTube world aspire at the moment.

On YouTube there is a world of users who have created an empire behind their channel, so with the points indicated, you know what steps to take to achieve them all and realize your dream of making money with YouTube.

types of ads that exist on YouTube .

TRICKS TO IMPROVE YOUR YOUTUBE CHANNEL

YouTube is not only a video platform but it is also the second most important social network of the present and safe of the future. Any company that wants to promote itself in networks is essential to create and promote your YouTube channel in order to increase your visits and generate a better return on investment for your business company or personal brand.

1. Optimize your content on your YouTube channel to have a good SEO

YouTube is not just uploading a video and that's it. You need to do an SEO process to make your channel visible.

The YouTube algorithm takes into account many factors to make your channel more visible against competing videos. To do this you need, first of all, to choose the basic keywords that you will have to implement in order to be able to implement them in the names of the video files that you upload, in the titles, descriptions, tags, annotations, playlists with keywords, etc.

2. Create very good titles for your video

Something very important is to create a good title for your video, and not precisely chosen at random, but by doing a keyword research with free tools such as google keyword planner or KWFinder or with payment tools such as Sistrix or Semrush

The title of your video on YouTube should call the action and also be an informative title.

Click To Tweet

Your title should not be extensive but direct with what you have in that video. I give you an example so you can understand it better.

Checkout an optimized title and another not so well optimized:

Optimized: 3 Actions to improve the CONVERSION of a digital business, with Ricardo Tayar.

Not Optimized: Conversion actions of a digital business.

In the first case, I not only made a call to action listing the actions that will be counted in the video but also capitalized the word that I consider key in the video and also named the author of this video.

In the case of the not optimized, it can be seen that it is a much more generic title, that does not attract attention like the other and does not invite you to click on it to visualize it.

3. Create clear and attractive YouTube thumbnails

Although YouTube gives you to choose 3 thumbnails to choose from the video, they may never reflect what you want to capture with them and you will not get interaction with them. The thumbnails are a fundamental part to get the click and I will tell you the steps to follow to be able to have some great custom miniatures.

Create mini-hooks that hook and make the viewer interested in your content.

Click To Tweet

The importance of Clickbait on YouTube

Clickbait is that "cyberanzuelo" that makes your thumbnail image attractive to the user and click with your mouse on your video. There are good and bad clickbait. The bad thing is that the thumbnail does not correspond to the content of the video but it does make you enter it, but later ... when you see that its content is not what it promised, you will leave this video. The opposite is the good one, that the thumbnail not only corresponds to the video but also to the title of the video, everything has a coherence and makes you finally watch that video.

Think that the thumbnail will look a fairly small size , even less if viewed from a mobile device therefore, do not use many letters and less in an illegible size since they will not be visible and people will not click on your video. It should also reflect the content of this video.

miniaura youtube

Tips for creating thumbnails: The close-ups of the face work very well, large texts with brightly colored backgrounds, contours in letters or silhouettes making the image more dynamic.

YouTube mini-books must have a resolution of 1280 × 720

Click To Tweet

Make sure you upload your thumbnails with a maximum size of 2MB and in .JPG format

4. Fill in the keywords of your channel very well, verify your account and complete all your data in your profile

Make your channel like a home. That is, that people enter your channel and everything is well structured, with everything well optimized, your profile picture is optimal, your background is well trimmed so that it looks correct on all devices and generates a good description and trailer in your channel.

The description of your channel is the cover letter, the first thing a user sees when entering your channel, do not miss this opportunity and start well from the beginning.

Include links to your social networks

youtube cover

It is very possible that people who watch your videos are interested in getting into your social networks. Make it easier by indicating all these social networks . I tell you in a little trick so that the name of your entire website appears as it appears in the photograph above.

It is possible that in the new version of YouTube does not let you change the links or enter them from scratch, therefore go to the old version from the top right on your profile and select the last option that is to go to the previous version of YouTube. From there follow these steps:

youtube channel

Click on the cogwheel and check that you have active the option "customize the design of your channel"

Thanks to this enabled option you will be able to visualize the option of links that will be shown where you previously changed the background image on your channel, that is, on the top right, click on the pen and click on «edit links. There you will arrive right at this screenshot

YouTube profile

As you will see in the first option it is the only one that will appear all the text, so instead of putting «web» put your web directly without the http: // as it appears in the image and so you can show your web in a way Visual much better.

5. Do not disconnect and stay active in your channel constantly

Not only worth uploading a video and waiting for likes and comments. Those likes and comments will come up when you generate that necessary interaction with your audience. Respond to comments on your videos and comment on other people's videos that are references to you. With this you will make your audience much more committed to you.

Have people subscribe to your channel and do not forget that "hit the bell" that is, not only activate the subscription to your channel but also activate the alert for when you upload a new video. This notice is located right next to the subscription button.

The constancy on YouTube is a fundamental factor to grow your audience.

6. Use the Lead Magnet technique on your YouTube channel

There are different ways to capture customers in your channel but one of the best is through Lead Magnet or subscriber acquisition giving something in return. It consists of giving something valuable to your users in exchange for their email or subscription, such as Luis Villanueva , Neil Patel , Vilma Núñez or Javier Elices use this strategy and it works great. Of course, the content you offer has to be of value and oriented to your audience.

What can you offer in your Lead magnet strategy?

You can offer ebooks, a pdf guide of the video content so that they also have it in written format, templates to help the client in different billing services, design, events etc ...

To do this you must generate calls to action (CTA) of different types such as creating an entradilla and an end in your videos that encourage you to download the gift in the description of the video itself or also generating a card on YouTube inviting people to subscribe

Insert a link from your Lead Magnet at the beginning of your video description

Once you've generated this Lead Magnet, don't just put it on your YouTube channel. Move your video through social networks such as Facebook, Twitter, Instagram or Linkedin and you will see how constancy will start your followers to grow.

7. Use Adwords as a tool to generate audience

You can make your video come out related to other videos through the Google Adwords Discovery option, with this advertising you will allow the user to click on your video. The other option is called trueview, it is the option in which your video will be launched at the beginning of the visualization and that the user will be able to spend 5 seconds even 30 seconds. That is, if the client clicks to exit the video before those 30 seconds it will not count as a visualization.

This advertising is great to generate Branding for your brand, you may not convert if you sell a product but what you will do and at a very economical price is to generate that visualization of your service, product or personal brand among others.

8. Generate a post of your own video

A very good option is to be able to generate a post by transcribing your video and giving valuable content on your blog. With this you can give a new written and valuable content, complementing your video with valuable content. Not only can you do it in this order but you can also generate a video from a post you made earlier. Take advantage of this opportunity and create new keywords positioned in your blog and increase the time spent by inserting the linked video in your post.

inserting a video in your blog you will gain time of permanence.

Click To Tweet

9. Generate playlists

By generating playlists on your channel you can make your users consume one video after another. Not only will you be able to insert videos from your channel into this list, but also related videos from other channels and influencers, creating variety in your lists and making it possible for anyone interested in similar videos from your industry partners to reach yours as well.

With the playlists you can also position your videos because by generating these lists you enrich the keywords and help the YouTube search engine to position your content.

10. Use final screens and cards in your videos

Use final screens

they will appear in the last 20 seconds of your video and keep in mind that to insert final screens, your video must have at least 25 seconds. The final screens will encourage new subscriptions and also new views to other videos.

YouTube gives importance to generate these final screens, therefore take this opportunity and think before generating the video, that is, in the edition, and leave those seconds later to be able to generate your final screen in the video.

Imagine that you forget to leave those final 20 seconds in your video and you are explaining with a Screencast something important and just two videos are placed as final screens and make the content of your video is not visible. Therefore it is essential to think about that time and in the edition place a previously created screen for these final screens, here I show you an example:

Final score   Final Screen

Reserve in the edition of your video the last 20 seconds to insert your final screens

Use cards in your video

With this option you will create links to other videos or playlists, you can promote your channel, do surveys and also link your website. These options, both the final screen and the cards are visible from mobile and are configured in the edition of each video. I leave a screenshot where you can see exactly where these menus are located for configuration.

11. Partner with other youtubers

If you want to grow on a YouTube channel is to be able to partner with other youtubers , but you may wonder ... how can I approach them? You will have to be especially original, and why not ... Generate a video and address that person privately, offer your services, your tutorials or simply thank the work you are doing, create a link with this person or company and you will make it possible for He also looks at you and if he likes what you do he can help you in different ways. .

If this option comes out it can be a great strategy to increase your reach and create new subscribers.

12. Use original and royalty-free songs

A fundamental error when starting a YouTube channel is to insert in your videos, known songs protected by copyright, this is not a correct action since you not only run the risk of your video being blocked, but even if it is not blocked, rest assured that you won't be able to monetize it.

You never know if a video of you can grow on visualizations or be sponsored, therefore, my advice is to always use royalty-free songs. You have many pages that allow you to have these options, even YouTube itself allows you to choose from thousands of songs prepared to monetize your videos and of course, royalty-free. You can find it in your menu at the bottom left in the "CREATE" section.

13. Use YouTube analytics

Analyze the content of your channel, see the visits you receive, where they come from, how old are your followers and an endless number of tools that YouTube offers for free within your channel, specifically on the left side "analytics" you can see the viewing time of each video, and something very important, the retention of the audience. Fundamental parameters to know what video works and learn from your audience to improve your statistics.

CHAPTER FIVE

TWITTER MARKETING 2020

Twitter has over three hundred million active users monthly and a young user base that boots, Twitter is a great platform for most marketers.

Setting up a company Twitter page is quick and easy to setup. All you need is to upload a profile picture, fill out a bio, and send the first tweet. However, not so simple is to expand your Twitter account, turn it into a real tool, get leads and build your brand.

To increase the number of real followers on Twitter, it's not enough to send a tweet whenever a company releases a product or holds an upcoming event. Interact with your target audience and interact with them. Successful Twitter marketing is powerful. If you become a professional on this fast-paced social networking site, you will gain new opportunities to grow your business online.

Twitter differences

The approach to all social media sites must be different. For example, Twitter's marketing strategy is different from Pinterest and Facebook's marketing plans. Understanding how Twitter works and where it fits in the social media environment determines how you use Twitter.

The main ways companies use Twitter are:

- Sharing information and content

- Promote engagement in promotional activities

- Interaction with consumers

- networking

- Increase brand visibility

All these are related to interactions. For example, it's not just broadcasting content like Instagram and Pinterest. Twitter makes communication successful. Keep this in mind as you continue the rest of this guide and delve into the heart of Twitter marketing.

Beyond the tips on "Setting up your profile correctly" and "Following influencers". Learn about the actual Twitter marketing strategy to be more successful and the steps necessary to do professional marketing. If you are interested in how to market your business on Twitter, keep reading.

Twitter chat: Undeveloped market

For years, marketers have asked the question "How can I increase my Twitter followers?" The question I really want to ask is "How can I increase my active Twitter followers?" The answer is Twitter chat. I have been promoting Twitter chat for quite some time. It's great to see a lot of marketers gradually starting to recognize the power of Twitter chat when it comes to getting positive followers.

The reason why Twitter chat is so effective is that people who participate in Twitter chat enjoy active participation in social networks. It is not just used for content distribution and consumption. Instead, these people use Twitter for the intended purpose, that is, to interact. These are the types of users who respond to tweets, retweet content, or expand messages.

To get started, look for industry-related Twitter chat. Whether you are in the marketing industry or are targeting business owners and entrepreneurs, Chloe West has compiled a great resource for the latest Twitter chat on topics such as content marketing, social media, and business. You can also use Google at any time.

Can't find an industry Twitter chat? Let's start by yourself. The key to success in Twitter chat is to be more than an audience. You need to add value to the conversation and differentiate it. Using tools such as Canva, you can create beautiful Twitter images very easily within minutes.

Canva social media image size

Another tip to gaining loyal followers during Twitter chat is to reply to other chatters. Most of the tweets must be in reply to others. Don't forget to @mention to receive notifications. Finally, follow up on the new connection you created during the chat.

Create a Twitter list for each participating Twitter chat and add the participating users to the list. Then start retweeting, posting to favorites, replying to tweets, and sharing content. Make sure that the relationship does not disappear after the Twitter chat ends.

HOW TO LEVERAGE TWITTER AS A MARKETING TOOL

How to use twitter as an Online Marketing tool?

Twitter online marketing Twitter is one of the best known and most important social networks after Facebook. So what we have to ask ourselves is: How to take advantage and use twitter in our favor is to say, to loyalty, profitability our business or company? . Twitter has surprised the world with its exponential growth and its ability to keep millions of people connected tweeting 24 hours a day, every day of the week and throughout the year.

It has a worldwide reach , you can follow favorite people, friends, mentors, etc. wherever they go and know what they are doing almost in real time. You can also use Twitter to increase your sales, get customers, branding your company as a professional.

Using Twitter as an online marketing tool will help you expand your business or company. The nature of Twitter is perfect for promoting your business due to the speed with which you can literally deliver your message to millions of people and around the world.

To launch an online marketing campaign and virally you only need a laptop and / or a PC with an Internet connection, it is no longer necessary to have a laptop but you can do it from your smartphone or iPhone . As you will see, marketing and the way of communication has changed radically in recent times.

Knowing how and why viral marketing works will help you understand when you use Twitter. In a nutshell, the theory is that you send a message (tweet) to your friends list about something you are doing at the time. The process is that they will send a Retuit "RT" to their lists or to their contacts and so on until thousands of people see your message. There are hundreds if not millions of people to respond to any call to action you have proposed in your message, such as "Find out here", "Enter Now", "Click", etc . There are good chances that some of those people were called to buy your service or product, all thanks to this Twitter Social Network.

When using Twitter as an Internet marketing tool or online marketing , you have to keep in mind that, due to its nature, your messages must be updated and frequently. With each message that is sent, the effectiveness of viral marketing tends to decline, so YOUR CONTENT must be INTERESTING and HIGH IMPACT to keep people's attention. Beyond this, it is one of the most effective ways to Do internet marketing.

Do you need to promote your product or service? Twitter is one of the most suitable tools for this. It is proven that Twitter is growing very fast and is giving a lot to talk around the world and everywhere. This works very well, but as in everything it is essential that you know how to use it correctly to be successful when marketing for your business or company.

MARKETING ON TWITTER IN 2020

Basics to better understand Twitter

What would a definitive guide be without the basics! Here is a short glossary so you can better understand this post and go hand in hand. ☺

Hashtag: Word that can be directly searched for your results by clicking. Usually, they are popular words or short phrases. They use the # symbol.

Lists It is a group of selected accounts that groups their content.

Mentions Way in which another user is called by tagging it. It is also considered a mention in response to some other person's tweet.

Direct message: Private messages that you can send to another person.

I like it. Heart shaped button to the right of a tweet. It serves to assess the content of the profile.

Retweet: Tweet from another profile that you forward to your followers.

Follower: Account that follow your profile to receive your tweets on your timeline.

Following: They are the people that you follow from your profile and you can see their tweets in your chronology.

Timeline Chronology of the tweets that generate the profiles you follow in real time.

Trending: Topic Popular themes or hashtags at the time of consultation

Tweet: It is an element composed of text, images, GIFs, videos or URLs.

BENEFITS OF USING TWITTER FOR YOUR COMPANY

There are many benefits that small, medium and large companies obtain when using Twitter. The main one is that it creates a direct and fast communication channel between your company and your current clients.

I share some of the benefits of Twitter for any company:

Benefit from trends. Twitter lets you know what the relevant topics your audience is talking about. It will allow you to participate in a useful way among your followers. For example, if you have a hotel and you see that in the trends there is a hashtag like #HoyPuedo, write a tweet where you include the trend: "#Today I can relax in the pool" and add a photo of the hotel pool.

Offer customer service. According to Twitter, for 85% of followers of small businesses on Twitter, it is relevant that they offer customer service from this social network. Following the example of the hotel, through Twitter you can promote discounts or packages, respond to comments and doubts that are generated or even generate reservations.

Create relationships with potential customers. Start or participate in conversations that are of interest to your company and create connections that may be something else in the future. Returning to the example, if you find conversations with related topics such as vacations, hotels or rest, you can interact in that conversation by inviting them to your hotel.

Increase the reach of your brand. Use your company's profile to increase the reach of your brand. If you have already optimized the profile with hotel data, location, telephone and logo, start interacting with profiles outside your community.

COMMON MISTAKES THAT ARE MADE ON TWITTER

The most common mistake in any social network is when you do not finish editing your profile.. There are many reasons: because it is lazy to finish it, because they want to go straight to tweet or just because it is a requirement of something without needing to use it. If you don't add your logo as a profile picture, nobody will know you. If you don't add a biography, they won't know what your company is about.

Follow and not interact. It will be inappropriate to use your Twitter account to tweet and follow people only without interacting with them. Remember, quality is better than quantity, followers who interact with you and share your content.

Get followers desperately. Or better known as the #followback and demand that they follow you. It is also a common mistake to buy followers, they will not add value to your profile and would denote distrust of observing a massive number of followers but that there is no mutual interaction.

Steal other people's content. Give a bad impression of your brand and image, as well as distrust. Take a moment to create your content according to the strategy you chose.

Fight. It doesn't matter if they are attacking your brand or someone made a claim response for your product or service. Provide kind answers and give a solution to your problem.

Use your account as spam. You can promote your brand but so that Twitter does not consider your spam account - or users report to you -, share only 20% of your posts a day for the promotion of your brand.

Before you start, create your profile

Have you heard the saying "the first impression is never forgotten"? Well, on Twitter for companies the profile is the first impression of your company or personal brand and yes, it is important and counts. I will show you the elements of a profile on Twitter and how to configure them to professionally show your company or brand.

Know the elements of a profile

To create your profile effectively, you must understand what elements make up a profile to tailor yours and generate a good impression.

Your user name. It is what users will identify you on Twitter. It can consist of up to 15 characters and goes after an arroba. The name you choose is with which users can search for you and mention you.

Profile picture. The photo is small, 400 x 400 px. Remember to choose an image that represents your company or brand as the logo. This image, besides being always visible on your profile, will be in every tweet you publish.

Biography. This is a brief description of you or the company as to why they should follow you. Always include basic information about your company such as location, hours or contact forms. In addition, it offers you the option of adding a link to your website.

Header Image Or also cover image, serves to highlight something you want to highlight the company visually. The image must have a size of 1500 x 500 px and can be a PNG image or a JPG.

Tweet set. It is a tweet that stays at the top of your timeline in your profile. It serves to highlight a tweet with important information and when people enter your profile do not miss it.

Once you understood the elements, start creating your profile.

What to tweet?

Hands to the keyboard! The time has come to tweet. 😉

The time has come to tweet

There is no specific rule for tweeting. You are free to write - only 280 characters stop you - and add the content you want in a single tweet. Nor is there a limit of tweets per day.

I can only give you some tips so that you get the interest of your audience when you tweet.

Write short tweets. Use a tweet for each message you want to convey. Be brief and specific.

Use visual content. You can add images, videos, GIFs and even live streams in a tweet. This type of content always generates interaction. You can include up to 4 images in a tweet.

Use the hashtags. They allow you to expand the reach of your tweet. Use hashtags that are relevant to your company or personal brand. I recommend using between 1 and 3 tags per tweet.

Make questions. Through the tool to create surveys -or with open questions in text-, you can launch questions of interest among your followers, that interact and even create conversations in the answers.

Answer Retweets. You can retweet some content of interest to your audience or your company or personal brand and write something when sharing it. In addition to generating content in your timeline, you can network with a retweeted user.

Interact The city of Rome was not forged in a day and neither will your community. The interaction will work as a tool to create loyalty between your followers and you , as well as an interest in your profile because you have shown interest in theirs!

Use of Twitter Lists for companies

A Twitter List is a group of accounts that you select in order to have a timeline with only the content of those accounts. The Lists can be created from your account or subscribe to Public Lists of other users. In case you create your own list, you decide whether to make it public or private.

The Lists will help you segment the people you follow a little more in detail and you can interact with them better.

HOW TO CREATE YOUR LIST ON TWITTER

1. Click on the "profile and configuration" button .

Step 1. Profile and configuration2. From the drop-down list, select Lists .

Step 2. Select Lists

3. Create a list on the "Create new list" button on the right side.

Step 3. Create new list

4. Add a name to the list and if you wish, a short description.

Step 4. Add a name to the list and a description

The name of the lists has a maximum of 25 characters. Choose a name that highlights what those profiles have in common. For example: Influencers, journalists, friends, etc.

5. There are two privacy options : the public one where users can see your list, who they are and even subscribe to it. In the private option only you can see the list, its content and nobody can subscribe.

Step 5. List privacy

6. Once the list is saved, start adding users to your list from the search engine or from the people you follow. ☺

Step 6. Search for users

To add people to the list

7. Continuing the previous steps, now look for the users you want to have in the list. For example, I look for influencers.

8. Found the profile, click on the 3 points .

Step 8. Click on options

9. In the drop-down menu choose the "Add or remove from a list" button .

Step 9. Add or remove list

10. A drop down will show with a list of the lists you have created. When you select the list, it is automatically added .

Step 10. Select list

11. Ready! You already have users on your list. When you enter the list, the user's activity will appear.

Step 11. Review the list tweets

Twitter Analytics

Twitter Analytics helps you measure, analyze and understand the growth in the number of followers, tweets and Twitter Cards. Each of the data analyzed by Twitter Analytics has its control panel and it is possible to download the information in spreadsheets for manipulation.

To access Twitter Analytics, you must click on the "profile and configuration" button of your account and click on "Analytics".

TWITTER ANALYTICS

Next I mention the data that each control panel handles according to what you want to analyze.

Twitter Analytics for followers

If you plan to measure the followers you have, Twitter Analytics helps you get relevant and specific information about them , such as their interests, location and demographic data.

The information is handled graphically with the following information:

Interests

Location by country and city

User sex

To access this information, in Analytics, click on the "Audiences" tab. Make sure that in the box below your profile information, select "His followers".

Twitter Analytics for followers

Analytics for tweet activity

Twitter's analytical tool works to measure the interaction and activity of your tweets , as well as general data.

In the control panel you first find general interaction data: mentions, profiles that have followed you, as well as those that stopped following you during the month.

After this information, you will find detailed information about your tweets such as the type of tweet that has the best response from the audience, the hours with the best reach and the number of clicks it has. The analysis is accompanied with basic information such as number of RTs, Favorites and the answers that were obtained.

Knowing the information of the activity will serve to know what content your audience likes best.

If you want to have all this information at your fingertips, go to Twitter Analytics and click on the "tweets" tab.

Analytics for Twitter Cards

It is the most important data to analyze in Twitter Analytics because it provides information to improve the content of the tweets that handle any of our links and get more traffic to the website.

To visualize and analyze the information, we can choose between seeing the number of clicks in the URL of the tweet or the number of Retweets. You can modify all this information in the control panel.

In the case of Twitter Analytics, it does not matter if the account has a long seniority, since the profile data is obtained from July 2013.

Twitter Ads

Twitter also has its ad service like other powerful social networks. You can search for recognition, interaction or clicks. To be clear, Twitter Ads only promotes and advertises on Twitter - not like Facebook Ads where you can promote on Instagram.

If you ever dare to use Twitter Ads, I show you the goals you can achieve.

Recognition and scope

Interaction in the tweets

Get followers

Promotion of a website

Apps Promotion

The goal they use most in Twitter Ads is recognition and reach. Maybe you handle topics of interest, your profile is very well optimized and the only thing missing is a push with ads for your account to take off. ☺

To access Twitter Ads, you just have to go to "profile and settings" and click on "Twitter Ads".

How to access Twitter Ads

Quick Promote

It is an extension of Twitter Ads where you can promote a tweet faster with a wider audience and in fewer steps.

This type of promotion is used specifically for content that needs to be promoted at the moment.

The situations where it is used are as follows.

Product promotions for a limited time

Tweets live from an event

Users with high interaction rate

Images taken at the moment

To enter is very simple, just go to "profile and settings" and you will find the Promote Mode option.

Twitter Ads and quick promote

Twitter Cards

Twitter Cards are tweets in the form of cards where it presents relevant information such as title, summary, user and image. Twitter Cards are free, you just have to be registered in Twitter Ads.

Example of a Card to promote web page

Many users don't know Twitter Cards, but they should. Here some advantages.

Improve brand image

Increased visibility

Better reach

Increased interaction

Highest response number

Higher CTR

Use of Twitter cards

These are the 4 uses that you can give to benefit the profile of your company or your personal brand.

Generation of potential customers. Similar to Facebook ads to generate leads, capture data from users interested in your product.

Websites. The card presents relevant and summarized information on the website, including the website link to generate traffic.

Basic applications. Promote applications for mobile devices.

Image application The same previous use, only that an image is added to identify the application.

Where to create my Twitter cards for companies

Before creating your cards on Twitter for businesses, you need to know the number of your Twitter Ads account. To know them, you only enter Twitter Ads - previously explained - and in the URL you will see a code. That code is your account number for Twitter ads for companies, save it.

Twitter Cards homepage

Tools to maximize the benefits of Twitter for companies

Companies that seek to grow, invest heavily in tools that help improve the strategy and positioning of their account. I share a small list of the most used tools for Twitter for companies according to the most important actions.

To manage and monitor

Tweetdeck In addition to managing your account and programming, you can monitor different aspects in the same window. The best thing is that it is free and easy to handle.

Hootsuite The most popular tool for managing social networks. Unlike Tweetdeck, in Hootsuite you can monitor and manage many accounts at the same time. The good news is that there is a free version to start. ?

Buffer. Another of the most popular is a tool that helps you strategically program your content and shows you what your content has been with the greatest reach.

Audiense One of the most complete tools, where you can monitor your community, you can manage your followers, you can even know the best time to tweet and on what days .

For analytics

Tweetbinder This tool allows you to see complete information about your shared links, tracking the hashtags you are using and everything you need to know about your Twitter account.

Bit.ly. The statistics it can offer you about your tweets is all you need. Bitly goes beyond a simple URL shortener hehe.

Metricool It offers you information about the reach, interaction and growth of your audience. The way in which Metricool shows its analytics, allows you to compare that growth with previous periods.

To interactuate

Retweet Rank. More than interaction, this tool offers you a report of the interactions your tweets have had, and also influence on your audience.

Mentionmapp This tool is super useful to know with whom of your followers it is worth interacting more, that is, it shows you which accounts you have had the most interaction with.

To search Trending Topics

Tweepsmap Based on location, Tweepsmap allows you to see where your audience is concentrated and shows the best times to tweet, as well as trends. It is based on numbers and percentages.

Trendmap With the help of an interactive map, this tool teaches you the trends and hashtags that are being used all over the world - I repeat, everything.

My initial recommendation is Audiense. It is a tool that helps you monitor and analyze your audience, interact more easily with your followers and automate direct messages when someone starts following you.

HOW TO EARN MONEY USING TWITTER

Twitter has long proven to be an effective tool for marketing businesses. Marketing specialists are discovering that the platform can be used to generate revenue directly. If you are not sure how to make money with Twitter, these are some of the ideas that will help you.

Its founders or first investors are not the only ones who have made a profit with this social network. Countless people and companies have harnessed the power of social networks to create new income opportunities.

If you want to know how to make money with Twitter these are some unique ways to make money with Twitter through some examples and some of the best practices to carry out.

HOW TO MONETIZE IN MEDIA STUDIO

How to activate monetization in Media Studio

For more information about our video ad solutions, contact your Twitter account manager.

Click on the Monetization button located in the top navigation bar.

Click Account Information in the drop-down menu that appears.

Complete all required fields on all three tabs:

Direction

Payment method

Tax Forms

Click on the Ready tab to complete the configuration.

How to monetize videos

For more information about our video ad solutions, contact your Twitter account manager.

Click on a video from the Media Studio library.

Click on the Monetization tab .

Click the Monetize this video button .

Select the corresponding content categories in the Tag your content section (select up to 2 categories per video).

If you don't want certain advertising categories to appear in front of your video, you can select the number of relevant categories in the Exclude tags section

Tip

Reduce too much tags; This may restrict the ad that could relate to your video.

If you don't want certain advertisers to associate with your video, you can enter these usernames manually.

HOW TO SET DEFAULT MONETIZATION SETTINGS

For more information about our video ad solutions, contact your Twitter account manager.

Click on the Monetization button located in the top navigation bar.

Click Settings in the drop-down menu that appears.

Turn on the Monetize all new videos with In-Stream Video Ads option if you want all recently uploaded videos to be automatically monetized.

Select the corresponding content categories in the Tag your content section (select up to 2 categories per video).

If you don't want certain advertising categories to appear in front of your video, you can select the number of relevant categories in the Exclude tags section

Tip

Reduce tags; This may restrict the ad that could relate to your video.

If you don't want certain advertisers to associate with your video, you can enter these usernames manually.

Click on Save . All new multimedia content to be monetized will have this configuration associated.

How to view estimated earnings by video

For more information about our video ad solutions, contact your Twitter account manager.

Click on a video from the Media Studio library.

Click the More statistics button .

Select a date range with the filter located in the upper right corner (whose default setting is a 7-day display).

Scroll down to the Estimated Earnings section to see the amount earned during that particular date range.

How to view publisher payment information (total earnings)

For more information about our video ad solutions, contact your Twitter account manager.

Click on the Monetization button located in the top navigation bar.

Click on Earnings in the drop-down menu that appears.

All payment information should appear, and be available for export.

CONCLUSION

In the world where more than 70% of internet users are involved on social networks, who spend at least one hour a day on social networks on average, we must infer that social networks have become a kind of reality in which people communicate, engage and, naturally, trust.

We also need to be aware that more than 60 percent of those users access social networks via mobile devices, with strong indicators that this percentage will only increase in the years to come.

In such a world, we have to admit that social networks are also part of the business world as a new dimension of reality. More than 90 per cent of advertisers say that they are or will use social networks for companies, while more than 60 per cent claim to have gained new customers via social networks.

The studies released by business professionals and advertisers support the fact that companies will benefit greatly from using social networks, which is why it has become part of business culture to incorporate such. That's why social media marketing is no longer considered on probation but has become an important part of the business world instead.

www.ingramcontent.com/pod-product-compliance
Lightning Source LLC
Chambersburg PA
CBHW052344220526
45465CB00003BA/943